# LONG BINH JAIL

*Road to Revolution*

*Code Number 72*

*The Craft and Crafting of History*

*Reason and Revelation*

*Guide to Images of America*

*Self-Destruction*

*Follow Me and Die*

*With Wings as Eagles*

*Edward Lansdale*

*For God and Country* (with Israel Drazin)

*Victory at Any Cost*

# LONG BINH JAIL

## AN ORAL HISTORY OF
## VIETNAM'S NOTORIOUS
## U.S. MILITARY PRISON

## CECIL BARR CURREY

**BRASSEY'S**
WASHINGTON, D.C.

*Diagram on p. viii by Molly O'Halloran*

**Library of Congress Cataloging-in-Publication Data**

Currey, Cecil B.
    Long Binh Jail : an oral history of Vietnam's notorious military prison / Cecil Barr Currey.
        p.    cm.
    Includes bibliographical references and index.
    1. Vietnamese Conflict, 1961–1975—Prisoners and prisons, American.
    2. Vietnamese Conflict, 1961–1975—Personal narratives, American.
    3. Prisons—Vietnam—Long Binh (Dông Nai)  4. United States.
    Army—Prisons. I. Title. II. Title: 1st ed.
    DS559.4.C87     1999
    959.704'37—dc21                                                99-23634
                                                                      CIP

ISBN 1-57488-186-8 (alk.paper)

Printed in the United States of America on acid-free paper that meets the American National Standards Institute Z39-48 Standard.

Brassey's
22883 Quicksilver Drive
Dulles, Virginia 20166

First Edition

10 9 8 7 6 5 4 3 2 1

FOR MY TEACHER SAMS:

Samuel Bowman Currey
Samuel Martin Hamilton

# CONTENTS

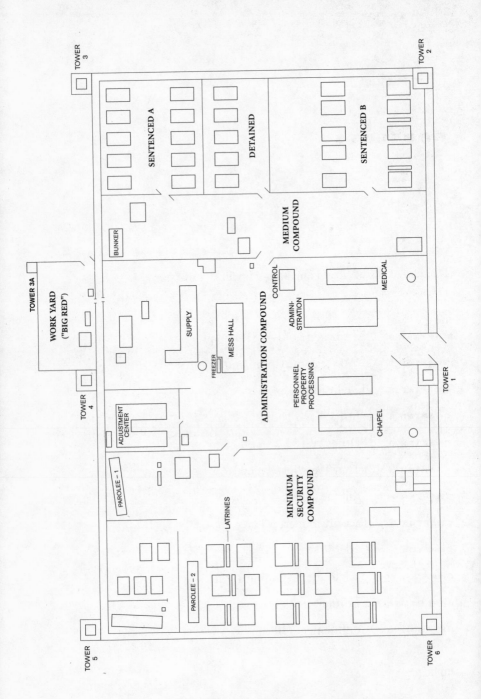

The U.S. Army Vietnam Installation
Stockade (USARVIS) at Long Binh

# PREFACE

This book is based on the best evidence it was possible to find. It grows from anecdotal reminiscences offered by those who were at the United States Army Vietnam Installation Stockade (USARVIS) at Long Binh and who thus knew it best. Through extensive research, I located and interviewed more than one hundred individuals whose words tell this story: dozens of inmates from every period of its operation, commandants (known properly as "confinement officers"), guards, chaplains and chaplain's assistants, social workers, legal officers, physicians and medical personnel from a nearby military hospital, general officer provost marshals, a computation clerk, a supply clerk, first sergeants, one who claimed to be a sniper/hunter assigned to track escapees, and others. For the most part, I have let them speak for themselves about their memories.

Former inmates were reluctant at first to reveal what happened to them there. When contacted, they were wary about questions dealing with those days and cautious about talking to a strange voice on the telephone. The same was true of those who were guards and staff. Until now most of them have been as silent about their experiences and as invisible to society as are those who died in that war. Yet, finally, almost everyone I spoke with opened up, sometimes releasing a cathartic rush of words.

Those who were inmates when they were nineteen and twenty years old still suffer and often continued to have brushes—or worse—

with the law. Conversely, many who served as correctional personnel are often still working in civilian law enforcement and penal facilities. Former guards are police. Former commanders came to head state prison systems in New York, Iowa, and Arizona.

Many former inmates, in their late teens and early twenties at the time described in this book, but now men close to fifty, are or have been incarcerated in civilian prisons and psychiatric hospitals, some intermittently, some almost continuously. Many live on the fringes of society, working in marginal jobs or unemployed. They cannot hold steady jobs. They never learned how to operate within the system. Many suffer from post-traumatic stress disorder (PTSD), and nearly all have difficulty functioning. For some, their hatred of what happened to them in Viet Nam remains clear and fresh. "I could never forgive what they did to me at LBJ," one man confided. "I swore then, and I swear today, if I ever again see that fucker of a guard I'll off him on the spot."

All too many former inmates at LBJ were later unable to establish normal relationships with others. They have abandoned, or been abandoned by, numerous women. They are fathers but are not in touch with their children. They are drug addicts or alcoholics. They choke on their bitterness. Some have tried suicide and committed violent crimes. They are damaged goods.

They have called me collect on the telephone after learning I was interested in their stories. My phone has rung in the small hours of the night as they have called from jails and prisons to relate some additional incident that came to mind or to ask for my help. They have sat with me at lunch counters and in bars, thousand-yard stares on their frozen faces. They have written me letters, the penmanship of some in a style reeking of schizophrenia. Their counselors at psychiatric hospitals have at times called to tell me how helpful it has been for them to unburden their souls. These men have asked me to write letters of support for their parole requests, to write to their mothers, to "loan" them money, to arrange for someone to "take care of" unfaithful wives.

Some of the stories they have told are generalizations, exaggerations, or braggadocio; some are outright lies cut from new bolts of cloth. This became clear when their accounts were checked against stories told by others. But if they had told their tales within the walls of a church, listeners would recognize their words—true in a literal sense or not—as a kind of testimony, sometimes a confession, and, almost always, an appeal.

Although the story of these men and that drab and fearsome military stockade is interesting of itself, we must not lose sight of the fact that the prison's very purpose was to reinforce a disciplinary hold on all GIs serving in Viet Nam and to punish those who would not, or could not, follow the rules. Former inmates described harsh conditions they hated and fought, but that the military imposed on them deliberately, as deterrents. Other GIs took due notice of what happened to miscreants who stepped out of line and accordingly avoided such behavior themselves.

Former inmates and former enlisted Military Police guards at Long Binh were not the only ones who were reluctant to talk with me. This was also the case with a few retired Military Police Corps officers. One former confinement officer comes to mind. He was concerned that I had not gotten "clearance" from the Department of Army to write this account. When offered the opportunity to comment by telephone on his tenure as confinement officer during the first half of 1968, he abruptly refused unless I first accepted certain of his demands for identification. That I was a university professor and a chaplain, an Army Reserve colonel with a top secret clearance, as well as an established author of several books, finally convinced him to write me a long, detailed letter spelling out his recollections of his time as confinement officer. I thank him for his efforts.

Retired Major General Karl Gustafon, Military Police Corps, was also initially reluctant, although he later cooperated gladly. Ivan "the Terrible" Nelson, retired colonel and former confinement officer, reacted by insisting that "I'd really prefer not visiting about the stockade," although he did consent to a brief, mostly unhelpful, interview. Former confinement officer Willy L. Jones laughed at such concerns. "That's amazing that they talk about getting clearance. What kind of clearance could they or you possibly be given? We're not dealing with a combat situation. We're dealing with a dang stockade! If there's anything classified about it, it's about someone being brutalized, and they don't want it to come out."

All who served in Viet Nam—enlisted personnel, noncommissioned officers, and officers—were under the authority of military rules and regulations. Those who broke these rules most often, however, were usually from the lowest ranks. Most of them had been drafted. Those who had a stake in the system, career officers or enlisted men, refrained from behavior that might bring on a court-martial.

Between 1965 and 1973, American boys from cities and farms left jobs and schools, most because they were drafted, and found themselves halfway around the world, living in an alien culture, fighting and sometimes dying in a cause that most at best only half-understood. Suspicion and fear were constant companions as they fought in the jungles of Southeast Asia. Violence was, for some of them, a daily experience. These low-ranking GIs carried out orders of those from above, bore the brunt of combat, and counted the days until their date of estimated return from overseas (DEROS), hoping they might complete 365 days In-Country and then, alive and uninjured, return home to try once again to lead normal lives.

These young American soldiers sought to avoid the double dangers of death or injury in their periodic encounters with soldiers of the Viet Cong's National Liberation Front (VC NLF) or khaki-clad members of the North Vietnamese Army (NVA). Imminent death was the worst threat, and danger was always at hand. Weather was a constant enemy, with the rain and damp rotting, mildewing, seeping into jungle boots, and pelting against ponchos. They sweat during sunlit hours and shivered at night. Booby traps exploded with mindless violence. Sniper bullets found men quietly taking their ease. Midnight silences shattered as determined VC or NVA soldiers attacked U.S. fire support bases. Enemy rockets blasted at sandbagged emplacements. Ambush caught the unwary and the watchful alike. They repeatedly wandered over the same ground in endless patrols. They fought for real estate that was then abandoned after bloody losses. They saw enemy soldiers armed with weaponry and supplies sometimes "made in America." They saw their buddies "blown away," "wasted," or maimed. They were repeatedly warned they could trust no one—not the bar girl, nor the sidewalk peddler, nor the farmer. They must even be on guard against six-year-old children; some that young were armed and ready to kill.

The young Americans became part of the "Green Machine," a mechanism geared to attritional slaughter in order to satisfy their superiors who sought ever greater "statistical indicators of progress." Some enlisted men, forced into the military by the draft, found cynicism rotting their bellies and eroding their confidence in the honor and purpose of those who led them. They no longer believed the patriotic rhetoric of the men who asked them to risk their lives to achieve the noble goals of the United States. "It don't mean nothing" came to be their common utterance. In ever-increasing numbers as the war progressed, some of those private soldiers, out of fear, frustration, boredom, anger, and contempt, sometimes broke the rules set forth by their superiors.

Sometimes their resentment took mild forms. They stopped shaving. They went unwashed. They discarded parts of their uniforms, wearing only what seemed to them to be useful or needed. They stopped saluting or did so only in sloppy, insolent fashion. Lieutenants were the officers they saw most. LT was the military abbreviation for such a rank. Young men abandoned the old military address of "Sir" when they spoke to those officers, instead calling them "el-tee."

Or they penciled on helmet camouflage bands such graffiti as peace symbols, slogans such as "Re-up? I'd rather throw up," "Power to the People," "Kill a noncom for Christ," "No gook ever called me 'Nigger,'" and "The Army [or Westmoreland, or some other selected person or outfit] sucks." In the late 1960s and early 1970s, some GIs in Viet Nam chalked on their helmets the legend "UUUU": "The unwilling, led by the unqualified, doing the unnecessary for the ungrateful."

A powerful resentment built toward the Army, toward officers, toward even noncommissioned officers (NCOs), and continued to grow. Many young soldiers resorted to surliness, refusing to follow discipline. They made their way through their required year of service in Viet Nam by doing whatever was necessary to stay alive and no more. They excused their behavior by claiming, with some justification, that those who gave them orders lacked the talents, training, and character they needed to earn the respect of those they led.

Others, more desperate, went beyond relatively mild rebellion. They went absent without official leave (AWOL). Drugs were easily procured and quickly consumed to quell the uneasiness—and sometimes terror—that was always lurking just below the surface of their consciousness, in some secret corner of the mind. In enlisted ranks, use of marijuana and harder drugs became so common that it grew into a systemwide epidemic, contaminating even installations in Europe and at home. Some soldiers refused combat. They bought and sold and traded on the black market.

Then there was growing racial hatred. Black soldiers created an enclave within Saigon where they lived and relaxed during off-duty hours. Estrangement of the races became so grave that white military policemen refused to enter that area except when accompanied by armed convoys. Such hostile divisiveness went beyond Saigon. It extended into units across the land and, after courts-martial, into LBJ itself.

Still another source of trouble was the animosity between conscripts and "lifers." In many units, tension and hatred between these groups grew so strong that men fought not only with the enemy but among themselves. The term "fragging" came into the English language, derived from "fragmentation grenade." It described assaults, sometimes ending in death or mutilation, on NCOs and company-grade officers, by the men serving under them. For the year 1969, the Army admitted to at least two hundred documented fraggings. In 1970 it announced 363 such cases. Official admissions may well not have accurately reflected the number of such attacks. According to some reports, troops of the 101st Division (Air Mobile) offered a reward of $10,000 for the assassination of the officer who gave them the order to attack Dong Ap Bia, a mountain in the A Shau valley, a ten-day (10–20 May 1969) meatgrinder known to soldiers as Hamburger Hill.

Those trapped in the cauldron that was Viet Nam often suffered severe trauma. They served their year there. They did the deeds asked of them and sometimes more. Eventually they returned to the "World"—sometimes marked for life, although not all their wounds were visible to others. Their commanders went on to receive still more promotions.

Decades later many GIs are still touched by PTSD, caused by the sights and sounds they endured all those years ago. At the time, when possible, they tried to forget or ignore the insanity that surrounded them. It was the duty of NCOs and officers to seek out those who sought relief in some drug-induced mental lotus-land, to identify and arrest them. The military, after all, had rules about proper conduct and behavior.

The reward for military miscreants was confinement at Long Binh's military prison. Most who ended up there were enlisted men. Officers, with more at stake, broke the rules rarely and so had little to fear from the stockade at Long Binh. Few were ever consigned to the cells inside the cyclone fences and barbed concertina wire that formed its perimeter. The few exceptions were unusual cases. One group was composed of Colonel Robert Rheault and six fellow Special Forces officers, confined there in 1969 for allegedly killing a Vietnamese double agent. After an initial furor and much publicity, charges against them were dropped.

Not even that many noncommissioned officers served time at Long Binh Jail. The inmate population was essentially made up of enlisted men holding the rank of private, private first class, or specialist fourth class at the time of their arrest. Courts-martial judgments usually reduced them to the rank of private prior to their arrival at Long Binh Jail. They were in their late teens or early twenties, and they were the ones who paid for their infractions.

Every soldier assigned to Viet Nam detested the name LBJ. It was the most hated place in the combat zone, always a brooding presence in the lives and consciousness of young soldiers. Fear of being sucked into its coils kept many an unwilling, and sometimes unruly, American soldier on the path that is called narrow and straight. It was such a feared element of military mythology that the simple threat of being sent there was sufficient to keep many GIs obedient to orders. They would rather face the enemy than serve time at LBJ.

Many of those sentenced to serve time were incorrigible "discipline-busters," repeat offenders. They had run afoul of superiors, NCOs and officers both, time and again. They had refused military orders or had abused drugs or gone AWOL, hoping to lose themselves in the general populations of such cities as Nha Trang, Hue, Da Nang, or Saigon. They had assaulted someone in a position of higher authority. The worst were those convicted of murder or rape or who had been convicted of war crimes. Apprehended and arrested by Military Police, they were taken to be tried before stern-faced officers sitting as judges in a military tribunal. At the end of their trials, as they stood at attention to hear their sentences pronounced by the president of the court, they heard the fearsome words: "Guilty as charged on all counts. Remanded to Long Binh Jail." And so they were then taken, under escort, to the admitting gate at Long Binh Jail and introduced to life in that facility.

Inmates there were watched over by a variety of people. Except for men on temporary duty, detached from nearby units to work for a time at Long Binh Jail, most of those assigned to the compound were members of the Military Police Corps, whether enlisted men, NCOs, or officers. Some who provided special services came from other branches, such as the Medical Corps or the Chaplain Corps. Lawyers belonged to the Judge Advocate General Corps (JAG). The bulk of those who worked at LBJ, however, belonged to the MPs. The supervising officer was known as the confinement officer. Under him was his deputy and a headquarters section. Other sections included supply, operations, communications, mess facilities, medical and dental services, counselors, personnel, a chaplain's section, and others.

The gravest burden fell upon the largest group of supervisory personnel within the wire: guards who had the most contact with inmates. They regularly worked twelve-hour shifts, six (and sometimes seven) days a week. They administered discipline, watched inmates always both in their cells and while they were on work details. They accompanied prisoners to sick call, to meetings with lawyers, to church services. Their presence was ubiquitous. Much of the story that follows grew from the recollections of these men.

———

By its nature an oral history falls short of the goal once set by historian Leopold von Ranke, who wanted to tell history exactly as it happened *(wie es eigentlich gewesen war)*. Perhaps no historian can achieve that, but the author of an oral history has a distinct set of problems with which to wrestle. His sources do not necessarily tell what happened but what is remembered. The tale grows from and relies on the memories of those interviewed. Some readers may remember the musical *Gigi* written by Lerner and Lowe. In that production Maurice Chevalier and Hermione Gingold sang a wonderful song, "I Remember It Well." Both were recalling the same event, but their memories diverged. "We went *here.*" "No, we went *there.*" "You wore *this* dress." "No, I wore *that.*" "Ah, yes, I remember it well." But they didn't. The point of the song was that the passage of time makes people forget, and that memory itself can be selective. Our memories are shaped by our perceptions and our personalities.

The Army stockade in Viet Nam opened in 1965 and was not closed until 1973. More than twenty-five years have passed; time enough for even the best memories to dim. These pictures of the past that we hold in our minds do not remain fixed after they're embedded in our brains. They constantly change; details are altered, added, and subtracted. We each create a version (and vision) of the past that is uniquely our own. So memory, while essential, is not an infallible guide to the past in any area, much less in constructing an oral history.

Participants in the same experience inevitably remember it from different perspectives. The same event may have each one involved at the center of that moment, yet each memory has differences ranging from large to small. Who is right and who wrong? Sometimes accounts can be harmonized, sometimes not. And what motives, explicit or implicit, guide the words of those with whom I have talked? Did they tell me what happened at LBJ? Or what they thought had happened there? Or what they wanted others to think had happened? Or what they wanted others to think they thought had happened? Those are four very different questions that readers must keep in mind as, in these pages, they encounter variations of the same events and experiences as seen by prisoners, guards, staff, and commanders.

———

Many people give of their time, experiences, and knowledge to an author during the writing of a book. My thanks go to all who were willing to be interviewed for this study. An appendix lists them by name and identifies them.

Particular appreciation must go to retired Lieutenant Colonel William Keyes, once a confinement officer at LBJ. He was always willing to talk, to recollect important information, to reminisce about his memories of the place, to speak frankly, and to supply me with the names of others with whom to talk. He was never too busy to help. My thanks go also to Mr. Joseph De Muro for providing me with helpful information and direction and to EG Custom Photographics in Tampa for generous assistance in preparing illustrations. Colonel David Parrish, Detention Department Commander, Hillsborough County Sheriff's Office, Tampa, Florida, was another who gave of his time to help me compare what went on at LBJ with methods used in modern jail systems.

I also thank Colonel Robert Swann, Office of the Staff Judge Advocate, Fort Jackson, South Carolina, for his careful reading of legal sections. I thank Dana Chwan for long hours spent in transcribing recordings of many interview sessions. Mr. Jack Crouchet provided invaluable help by supplying me with records from his old Viet Nam files, including a number of DA 2823 forms ("Witness Statements") that told aspects of the August 1968 riot at LBJ as seen and experienced from the point of both staff and inmates.

The U.S. Army Crime Records Center, Criminal Investigation Command, Falls Church, Virginia, helpfully supplied me with a one-and-one-half inch thick stack of Criminal Investigation Detachment (CID) forms DA 2823s, from which names had been deleted. They were helpful in setting forth my account of the riot. I am even more indebted to Jack Crouchet for searching his own files and sending me much the same stack of information that was still complete in every respect, with no names deleted. His material was of great help in my recounting of the events of the riot.

I am further grateful to George C. Deringer and Paul Grossheim, former confinement officers, and to retired Chaplain Vernon Swim for supplying me with photographs of LBJ that appear as illustrations in this book.

I would be greatly remiss not to thank a former student who studied with me in the late 1980s, Jodie (Johnson) Conover. In one of my seminars I assigned her the job of researching what she could learn about LBJ. Her careful and extensive investigative work was so well done that it pointed me in helpful directions as I began my own research, kept me from blind alleys, and suggested pathways to follow. I referred to it often in the early stages of my work and so, Jodie, you are a jewel, and I will always remember your help.

I thank Benton Arnovitz, Director of Academic Publications at the U.S. Holocaust Museum in Washington, D.C. He is a former editor of mine who first suggested this research project to me. My thanks go as well to my friend and former student Stephen Crane, Tampa Viet Nam Vets Center, for quickly and successfully researching the binoctal problem after so many others had thrown up their hands in despair. I also thank my agent, Joshua Bilmes of JABberwocky Literary Agency, and my editor, Don McKeon of Brassey's. They are good men to work with. Finally, as in my other books, I thank my wife of forty-seven years for her moral support and encouraging words.

Where appropriate in the following text, rather than constantly using *sic* to indicate even minor errors (something dear to the heart of academics), some capitalization, punctuation, and spelling in the interview transcripts have been changed to reflect proper grammar and usage, although dialect and style of speech have been retained. Obviously, any errors in this account remain solely my responsibility.

# CHAPTER ONE

# THE LEGEND OF LONG BINH JAIL

Jimi Childress, an African American, remembers well what happened that night of 29–30 August 1968 at Long Binh Jail in Viet Nam. He was a nineteen-year-old prisoner there, sent behind the barbed wire in February 1968 for about two months, released and then sent back again almost immediately, in April 1968, for a longer stay because he had gone absent without official leave (AWOL) from his unit. When he was interviewed in 1990 he was again a prisoner, number 7207, an inmate at Kansas State Prison at Lansing. But he remembered those days twenty-two years earlier and halfway around the world, where he first found himself behind bars.

INMATE PRIVATE JIMI CHILDRESS: "I was called 'Wild Bill' because I guess I was a pretty wild person at the time when I was in Viet Nam. We all had nicknames for one another and that's what the guys called me, and I guess it stuck. I know everything about what happened at the riots. . . . There was myself and four other guys and we just got fed up with the way we were being treated. Living in tents. Goin' out in the sun. Fillin' sandbags all day and bein' kicked around. So we decided to storm the place at a certain time at night."

What events led Childress to decide to do such a thing?

INMATE CHILDRESS: "I can recall that at one time they had eight of us in one conex box. A slit in front and a slit in back—and that was your air. And if you wanted to urinate, you had to go to the back to do it because they kept a chain on the front with a lock on it. This was in heat of more than 115 degrees. I can recall the monsoon season. We would have floating water. No place to sit or lie down. And this went on for days and weeks. . . . When the guards would finally let you out, you would be so humiliated, so angry, you would just have a hateful attitude. . . . You could about see them treating *prisoners* that way, but not their own soldiers.

"I can recall a time when they had me on . . . raw potatoes, a cup of water, and two or three pieces of Vietnamese bread. The only way I survived was that guys who did the cleaning up around would throw me an apple or orange or peanut butter sandwich . . . ."

Childress claimed that one of the black guards who worked on a watchtower in the area where Childress was housed was sympathetic to him and other black inmates. He provided the spark that set off the riot.

INMATE CHILDRESS: "I was the one who talked this guy into bringing in drugs. . . . After the riot they had me labelled as an instigator—which I was—a helluva instigator—I was one of the main instigators . . . . This guy brought in two or three bags of Binoctal pills and two or three bags of marijuana and he gave them to me.[1] This guy—I don't know his name and if I did I wouldn't say it—he brought that stuff in when he came on duty. He threw it over to me earlier that day . . . when he came on duty . . . about five or six o'clock when they change[d] shifts. It was about dusk-dark. . . . I went around and distributed it to a lot of guys."

Childress told those to whom he gave the drugs to listen for the evening whistles.

INMATE CHILDRESS: "What it was, we were behind a big fence and two [Military Police] guards would come in [at about dusk] and count [all of us]. When they came through all the tents and had completed their count and were proceeding back to the gate to go out, that's when myself and four other guys charged them. They blew

---

[1]Binoctal: The trade name for the quaalude methaqualone hydrochloride, a hypnotic and sedative drug. Also known by abusers as "Number Ten," and sometimes "Baby San Number Ten." Because of abuse at home and by the military in Viet Nam, it is now illegal to use or possess and is no longer distributed in the United States.

their whistles. And when that happened, people came from *every-where*. I didn't realize there were that many people in there!"

Childress remembered the hours just before the riot began.

INMATE CHILDRESS: "Most of the guys were high off the pills and high off the marijuana and angry. . . . [Y]ou take two Binoctals and you think you're superman. Anybody! Take two and you think you can fly. And that was what was needed.

"There were no whites involved [in planning the riot]. I know who the leaders were. I forgot their names and even what some of them looked like—my memory's been destroyed—but there were no whites involved in setting that riot off. In fact, there were a lot of whites beat on during the riot 'cause some blacks took it out on them as well. They were just trying to get somewhere where they would be safe, running around like chickens with their heads cut off. They were in danger also. We were mad at anything that was white, you understand?

"What it was, it was a *hate* that a lot of blacks had toward whites, period. Bein' out in the boonies, seein' their friends killed, seein' it's a form of genocide, hearing of Martin Luther King killed. It was just a hatred of anything white. Then when the riot set off, when a white guy was seen, he was beat on like he was a guard. It wasn't anything *personal*, you know, but these guys just had this hate for white people. Halfway around the world, in jail. Back home they rapin' our mothers and sisters and hangin' our daddies. It was a hard time.

"Another thing that made it so hateful. All these people that was in these conex boxes were black. You see? White guys in the stockade had fringe benefits. We had *none*. It was just a *hateful* place. Hispanics stuck with blacks, just for safety reasons, but there was so few you hardly noticed. It was a *black* prison. I will *never* forget how many blacks were incarcerated at that stockade."

During the riot, inmates ran free throughout the stockade. They seized guards as hostages and beat them into submission. They attacked white prisoners and beat them. They seized the stockade compound and set out on a rampage of destruction. They burned buildings and tore down what they could not set on fire. They collapsed guard towers. Weaponless, they tore metal bunks apart and used bunk supports as weapons. Some grabbed lengths of wood torn from furniture or broken walls to use as clubs. They ripped down tents and torched the remains. They rampaged through buildings, scattering the contents and setting fires. They threw personnel records from files in the administration building into a pile and put a match to them. That later made it difficult for authorities to tell who was who, who was responsible and who was not. The confinement officer, Lieutenant Colonel Vernon D. Johnson, came inside the wire, trying to talk the rioters into surrendering. Waving his arms in excitement as he spoke to one group, he accidentally touched an inmate and, like a pack of angry dogs, the men set upon him, beating him with clubs and injuring him severely. Soon retired on a disability pension, Johnson never recovered from the effects of that night.

———

It was a fearsome place. Dennis W. Currey, a holder of two Purple Heart wound awards and a former platoon sergeant, never saw the compound. But he quickly heard of it. Currey was sent to Viet Nam as a private in 1968 assigned to the First Infantry Division. During the In-Country orientation at the 90th Replacement Depot at Long Binh after Currey's arrival in Viet Nam, the speaker threatened new troops, warning them that if they broke military rules, they would end up living in a conex container at the jail at Long Binh.

SERGEANT CURREY: "He told us about drugs, about killing civilians, about obeying superior authority, about doing only what we were ordered to do. We were to stay out of trouble. I left that meeting convinced that I was going to do whatever was necessary to avoid going there."

Currey returned to Viet Nam for a second tour in May 1971 and again heard warnings about Long Binh Jail at the 23d Replacement facility.

Staff Sergeant Lawrence C. Geiger backed up Currey's memories and spoke for most GIs.

SERGEANT GEIGER: "I delivered a prisoner to Long Binh one evening. I never spent any time there. I never wanted to, either behind the walls or on the outside of them. I heard lotsa nasty stories about that place. Most of them were true. I never wanted to have firsthand knowledge of what was going on in there. . . . Things happened there that don't normally happen in jail in this country, even in a military lock-up. It was different. The whole system was different."

A Military Police guard, Clifford Prosser, who worked at the stockade during 1971, added these words:

GUARD PROSSER: "Maybe LBJ was feared because it personified military corrections over there."

An inmate there in 1968 and a man still in trouble with American law put it this way. Speaking from the Nottoway Correctional Center in Virginia, Gerald Stovall described his experience.

INMATE STOVALL: "LBJ was a *torture chamber*. People in America would never have believe that Americans would treat other Americans the way they treat us at LBJ. . . . Out of the last nineteen years I've only had seventeen months on the street. The treatment here is no way I can compare to what happened at LBJ. No comparison! I may be in prison but I'm not *in fear of my life* everyday like I was there. . . . I've never felt here the fear I felt there. Nobody who was ever there can forget LBJ."

———————

Rule-breaking service personnel in Viet Nam came from all branches of the U.S. military. Marines were sent to Corps stockades at Da Nang or Okinawa, although a few spent time in custody at Long Binh as transient prisoners. Only in later years did the facility at Da Nang come under the supervision of Long Binh Jail. U.S. Navy sailors went to Okinawa or to the Naval prison at Portsmouth, N.H., although a few spent time in the Army facility at Long Binh. The same was true for the Air Force. Those in the Army were sent to the United States Army Vietnam Installation Stockade (USARVIS), but no one ever called it by that name. In the early years of the American presence there, when it was first activated on a former tennis court at Pershing Field, near Tan Son Nhut air field in Saigon, soldiers simply called it "The Stockade."

Both while it was located at Saigon and later at Long Binh, USARVIS was not intended for long-term confinement of military prisoners. Those with short sentences or guilty of less serious crimes did serve their time at one or another of those locations and then, after their release, returned to their own or other line units to complete their year in Viet Nam. Weeks and months served at USARVIS were lost time. They did not count toward the year that soldiers had to spend in Viet Nam, and so GIs had to make up all the days they had spent at the military prison before they could return to the United States. A great many other men, those convicted of the worst crimes, did not stay long at USARVIS. They passed through its gates only as transients, to be held for a time until transport was available to take them to long-term confinement in the United States Army Disciplinary Barracks (DB) at Fort Leavenworth in Kansas or elsewhere. The same had been true of the first facility at Pershing Field.

One of the early confinement officers was Captain Walter M. Shumway, whose rank was lower than one might expect for such a position. A later confinement officer, Lieutenant Colonel Eli Gardner, spoke of Shumway's rank.

LIEUTENANT COLONEL GARDNER: "It's not surprising that a captain initially headed the stockade. They didn't expect it to grow that much. It was small at the time; expected only a few prisoners. It grew."

It was Shumway's job to supervise the stockade, at the time only a holding facility for prisoners during their trials. After sentencing, they were taken back to the continental United States (CONUS) or to Okinawa to serve time.

Sam Mullin, a veteran of service with the Military Police, remembers the first facility, named after General John J. "Black Jack" Pershing. When he arrived in Viet Nam he was a thirty-two year old sergeant.

SERGEANT MULLIN: "Pershing Field was a [Vietnamese] sports club we took over. . . . It was a very small compound, maybe the size of a football field. . . . [T]he face of Pershing Field was directly at the entrance to Tan Son Nhut air base and directly across this very wide dirt boulevard was the 3rd Field Hospital of Saigon."

MP Guard Marion Powers remembers that Pershing was further away from Tan Son Nhut.

GUARD POWERS: "[T]he stockade was probably two miles from the airport."

GUARD MULLIN: "To our rear across a one-lane alley was a permanent ARVN [Army of the Republic of Viet Nam] base where the
ARVN red berets were stationed. . . . Its perimeter was covered by a
very close cropping of fairly mature trees with a lot of shrubbery and
brush at their base which, of course, we laced with barbed wire."

Mullin recalled that the compound contained two buildings.
"[W]e used [them] for headquarters. The MPs were all in screened-in
tents, sandbagged up to thigh high. Very comfortable. We had a hell of
a lot of MPs. We had the 716th in Saigon, a reinforced or overstrength
MP battalion—almost two battalions. They had responsibility for all
facilities in the city. [The 557th MP Battalion, to which Mullin was
assigned] was responsible for Pershing and [had] joint control operations with the ARVN next door and Air Force security at Tan Son
Nhut. . . . Our only real danger point would have been a frontal attack,
which never happened. We had sandbag emplacements built [but] we
never used them."

Guard Powers recalled other details. Men of the 557th MP Battalion had duties other than patrolling the stockade.

GUARD POWERS: "We'd rotate a week in the stockade, the
next week on river patrol with the Navy up and down the [Saigon]
river. . . . [T]here was a Buddhist temple at one end of the stockade on
the other side of the road and a small Vietnamese village behind it.
This village had a well. Both the MP and the stockade latrines were
right next to the fence not more than twenty-five feet from the well.
All the stuff from the latrines went right down into the [village] well.

"[Pershing Field Stockade was surrounded by] a double-wired
fence, about eight feet high, with towers on two corners, so you had
one tower guard who could look down two fence lines and the other
could see the other two. There was a sally port at the entrance with
a guard shack to the left as you went in. That's where prisoners
were frisked as they came back from work details. Going on into the
stockade there were tents, ten or twelve, that were on concrete slabs;
a mess tent; inmates' tents on slabs with cots inside.

"It was just an open stockade. There weren't levels of security.
There weren't a lot of violent prisoners. They were AWOLs or being
detained to go to other prisons, Leavenworth. . . . [It] was a rather

small unit, probably didn't have more than fifty or seventy-five prisoners at the time I was there in '66. [Later, after the facility was moved, the prison population grew with] more troops going AWOL, troops that had committed crimes like murder against their commanding officer or executive officer or first sergeant. The inmates . . . had gotten fed up with the field environment. Most were from combat units like the 101st, the 73rd, Big Red One."

Mullin, also assigned at Pershing, agreed with Powers's assessment.

GUARD MULLIN: "Our capacity was, I think 140. There were other small stockades in use. . . . There was the Marine stockade in I Corps; 16th Group had a stockade at Nha Trang. [At Pershing there were handball courts] which we used for DESG."

The acronym stood for "disciplinary segregation." Mullin was noncommissioned officer in charge (NCIOC) of the disciplinary unit.

GUARD MULLIN: "That was very enjoyable. . . . A handball court is an awesome psychological battering ram on anybody who had to go in there and sit with nothing to look at but white walls twenty feet away from him."

There were incidents. Powers described one.

GUARD POWERS: "About nine or ten o'clock one night the prisoners got happy, started singing and acting drunk. They were. They'd made hooch out of raisins they'd got from mess personnel. . . . After that we rationed the sugar and fruits that could be made into hooch."

Another occurrence was more sobering.

GUARD POWERS: "About ten or eleven one night, one of the guards shot a prisoner trying to escape. He'd cut through the first fence. The guard shot at him with his M-14 and hit him in the palm of the hand; blew two of his fingers off. We got him taken to the hospital. This incited the rest and they started rioting. We had our helmets and flak jackets on, gas masks and tear gas canisters. . . . The prisoners were throwing rocks. I remember getting hit a couple of times. . . . The stockade sergeant in charge that night tried to get them to settle down and stop throwing rocks. They decided to use tear gas and threw some canisters into the stockade. After thirty minutes or so a lot were subdued. Laid down on the ground and [things] quieted down. Several rabble-rousers [were] taken out of the stockade to some facility out at the air force base."

An inmate at the time recalled the same event.

INMATE PRIVATE VERNON SHIPPEE: "A GI tried to escape and the guards shot and blew off a portion of his hand. That wasn't right. Americans shooting at Americans. It started a riot. We burned tents, used whatever wood we could find. The prison population then was less than one hundred; most of us were involved. The guards just let us play ourselves out. LBJ grew out of this incident, for the Army decided to put up a better stockade."

Until the end of the spring months of 1966, the Military Police battalion that had general oversight for Pershing Field had its headquarters there and its responsibilities for the stockade were simply added tasks. Then, in the early part of the summer of 1966 the top brass decreed that larger quarters were needed for a more permanent stockade facility. Pershing Field was closed down, and a new site was selected. Sam Mullin recalled that the move was part of Operation Moose.

GUARD MULLIN: "There was a Senate committee in Saigon. Senator [Robert] Taft from Ohio was chairman and he reported that Americans were doing bad things to the moral fiber and character of the people of Saigon, which of course caused outrageous laughter. Undoubtedly true. So we were to move elsewhere."

And they did.

━━━━━━

Throughout history, armies have punished soldiers who have broken the rules by which they live and fight. They have always imposed decrees regulating behavior. Such regulations form the backbone of discipline. Obedience is rewarded with pay, with medals, with promotion and retirement. Those who break the rules suffer demotions, loss of pay, confinement, discharge, and sometimes, in rare cases, death. The laws that govern the establishment and operation of courts-martial and list inappropriate personal behavior within the United States armed forces are set forth in the *Uniform Code of*

*Military Justice (UCMJ)*. Military law, in the words of the *UCMJ*, "consists of the statutes governing the military establishment and regulations issued thereunder, the constitutional powers of the President and regulations issued thereunder, and the inherent authority of military commanders."[2]

The military's *Manual for Courts-Martial (MCM)* contains the *UCMJ*, printed as Appendix Two. The *MCM* is the military "bible" for the operation of a court of justice within the armed forces. Systematic codification of such rules within the American military dates from 1917 when the United States entered the Great War. The rules were revised and updated in 1921, 1928, 1949, 1951, 1969, 1984, and 1995. During most of the Viet Nam conflict, the operative *MCM* was the 1951 edition, which appeared during the Korean War. As a result of the later Viet Nam experience, the *MCM* was again updated in 1969.

The reach of military law is long, providing penalties for a multitude of wrongs. A partial list illustrates its scope. Soldiers are punished for fraudulent and unlawful enlistment, desertion, being AWOL, missing a troop movement, insubordinate conduct or showing contempt or disrespect toward superiors, assaulting or willfully disobeying superiors, conspiracy, cruelty toward and maltreatment of others, misconduct as a prisoner, failure to obey orders, mutiny or sedition, misbehavior before or giving aid to the enemy, and spying.

Penalties are also meted out for making false statements, for damaging, losing, or wrongfully disposing of government property, for resisting arrest or escaping afterwards, for drunkenness, for misbehaving while on guard duty, for malingering, for breaching the peace, for making provocative speeches or using such gestures, for murder and manslaughter, for rape and sodomy, larceny, robbery, forgery, maiming, arson, burglary, for illegal entry, perjury, writing a check with insufficient funds, for unbecoming conduct, and even for dueling.

In recent years drug use has been an ongoing and constant problem in the military, which has dealt with it in a variety of ways. In the most recent *MCM* (1995), an entire section, Article 112a, of the *UCMJ*

---

[2]*Manual for Courts-Martial* (Washington, D.C.: U.S. Government Printing Office, 1995), pp. I–1.

deals with the wrongful use and possession of controlled substances. It proclaims punishment for anyone who "wrongfully uses, possesses, manufactures, distributes, imports, exports, or introduces into an installation, vessel, vehicle, or aircraft any controlled substance. Such forbidden drugs include opium, heroin, cocaine, amphetamines, lysergic acid diethylamide [LSD], methamphetamines, phencyclidines, barbituric acid, marijuana, or any compound or derivative of any such substances."

This article was codified because of the grave drug problem that beset America's armed forces during the Viet Nam conflict. It was also drafted to deal with a void in military law in the face of an ever-increasing number of drugs in the years that followed.

The 1951 and 1969 editions of the *MCM* did not have such provisions. Drug use by service personnel during all of the Viet Nam conflict was punished under more general provisions such as Article 92 (failure to obey order or regulation) and 134 ("all disorders and neglects to the prejudice of good order and discipline in the armed forces, all conduct of a nature to bring discredit upon the armed forces, and crimes and offenses not capital, of which persons subject to this chapter may be guilty, shall be taken cognizance of by a general, special or summary court-martial, according to the nature and degree of the offense, and shall be punished at the discretion of that court.") Because drugs were readily available in Viet Nam and, increasingly worldwide, wherever they might be stationed, many GIs ran afoul of the military regulations and were consequently punished.

Miscreants can (then and now) be dealt with in several ways. For lesser offenses they can be punished by their local unit commander in what are called Article 15, or nonjudicial, punishments. This is also known as "company punishment." Penalties range from lecturing the soldier to restricting his movements, to fines, to reducing his rank. A culprit has to agree to accept Article 15 punishment before his commander can impose it. If he chooses not to do so or is charged with more serious offenses, he stands before summary, special, or general courts-martial convened by higher command authority.

Summary courts are convened by battalion commanders or higher-ranking officers and are rather simple affairs, in which the commander deals one on one with the accused. No lawyers, military or civilian, participate. The next level, special courts, are convened by battalion commanders or higher. At this level a military judge and counsel for the defense are allowed. Such courts-martial can punish an offender with up to six months' confinement and a bad conduct discharge. General courts, as the name implies, must be convened by a general. This is a full press military court with a judge, jury, counselors, recorders, and all the other paraphernalia of a civilian trial. Punishments handed down by these courts can range from bad conduct to dishonorable discharges, to prison sentences of up to life, to forfeiture of part or all of pay and allowances, and, in extreme cases, to death sentences.

Some within the armed forces are only rarely faced with charges brought against them under the *Uniform Code of Military Justice*. A person who decides to become a military officer has made a deliberate life-altering choice. Such people are commissioned after taking an oath to uphold the system they are about to enter. Although many serve only the minimum time, some claim it as a career and move from company-grade rank (second lieutenants, first lieutenants, captains) to field-grade positions (majors, lieutenant colonels, colonels), and some few achieve flag rank (brigadier general, major general, lieutenant general, general). They have come to like the challenges and rewards of the life of an officer and make the military their home. Noncommissioned officers follow a parallel path. They enter the service as privates. Liking the structure and discipline of the military and doing well in that system, after spending time in each of the lower grades of private and private first class, they move up the ranks to become noncommissioned officers—sergeants, sergeants first class, master sergeants, command sergeants major. Such persons are known as "lifers."

Having volunteered for the armed forces, those who aim to rise through the ranks learn quickly how to deal with the demands made upon them. They avoid situations that would put their careers at risk. They seldom come into conflict with the system of military justice and rarely face a court-martial or any other kind if disciplinary action.

The Viet Nam conflict involved a wholly different kind of soldier, one who came into the armed forces because of the draft. Although a significant number of young men voluntarily enlisted in those days, the military could not have functioned without the draft. Between 1965 and 1973, 2,215,000 young men received draft notices and suddenly found themselves an unwilling part of the Green Machine. Of that number, 563,000 received less-than-honorable discharges with 529,000 given administrative discharges and 34,000 imprisoned following courts-martial.[3]

Many draftees in Viet Nam were angry, resentful, and fearful. They had been transported to a far corner of the world to fight in a conflict they neither understood nor endorsed. As the war continued year after year, frustrations and rage within the lowest ranks grew exponentially. Some chose to provoke the system in ways small and large. A fraction of those rebels were the ones who were court-martialed for breaches of discipline or criminal behavior. They were the ones who became prisoners at Long Binh Jail.

Many of those confined to the stockade in Viet Nam actually were good soldiers. They had learned well, during the days of their stateside training, the lessons they needed to function effectively and efficiently as fighting men. On maneuvers in the field, whether the mission was for reconnaissance purposes or a search-and-destroy effort, they did what they had to do in exemplary ways and even received medals for their work. It was at stand-down time, when not on duty, that things went wrong. These young men had access to vice in undreamed measure: sex, alcohol, drugs, gambling. Temptation was everywhere, and at age eighteen or nineteen, those soldiers were not mature enough to resist completely or to pursue such pleasures in moderation. James Hatton, a man from Philadelphia who arrived in Viet Nam in 1966 and ended up in Long Binh is an example.

INMATE HATTON: "I was assigned as a point man in [a unit of] the 101st Airborne for nearly a year. . . . I was a good guy in the field, knew what I was doing and did it well. My troubles always came when we were back in base camp where alcohol [and other things]

---

[3]Jerold M. Starr, "Who Fought for the U.S.: The Lessons of the Vietnam War," (Center for Social Studies Education, 1988), p. 10.

got me in trouble. . . . I became a Buddhist while In-Country and also had several [Vietnamese] 'wives.' The guys in the outfit called me 'Buddha'. . . . I hated pulling details. When there was time away from field duty, I wanted to go to town, get drunk, get 'married.' So I was AWOL a lot.

"My colonel and the First Sergeant wanted to keep me, so they would give me Article 15s rather than court-martials. During that year I received . . . maybe ten to fifteen Article 15 punishments. In February 1967 I was given the first court-martial. We had come in [to base camp] for three days' stand-down. They wanted to put me on details. I went into town instead. Then the unit got orders to go back to the field while I was gone. They came into town to get me. I was drunk, wouldn't go back to the field, wanted some downtime. So they court-martialed me."

Hatton later received a second court-martial, not long before he would have returned to the States.

INMATE HATTON: "I . . . took an In-Country R & R . . . . Decided not to go back to the unit. When they picked me up they caught me with some marijuana on me, so I got another court-martial in October 1967 and sent back to LBJ. Didn't get out until February 1968. . . . Inside I smoked as many reefers—or more—as I had on the outside. Marijuana was always available."

Hatton and hundreds of others like him stepped outside the boundaries of military regulations and then found themselves locked in cells at Long Binh Jail.

# CHAPTER TWO

# "WE WELCOME COMMAND FAILURES"

How did those young American warriors come to serve in Southeast Asia from 1965 to 1973? What brought them to that time and place?

The United States' involvement with Viet Nam dates back many years. During World War II, the Vietnamese revolutionary leader Ho Chi Minh worked with members of the U.S. Office of Strategic Services (OSS) to relay information about Japanese troop movements in Indochina and to return downed American fliers to safety in China. In return, OSS sent teams to help train Ho's newly formed military group in small unit tactics and weaponry. After World War II, however, any sympathy the United States had felt toward the communist government of Ho vanished, and Washington began to help France in its efforts to reestablish its colonial dominance in Viet Nam.

In 1950 the Pentagon established a command in Southeast Asia known as the United States Military Assistance and Advisory Group-Indochina (USMAAG-I). Its purpose was to provide assistance to the "forces of France." Following the 1954 defeat of French troops by Vietnamese forces at Dien Bien Phu and the meeting in Geneva of the Great Powers, MAAG-I was replaced by the United States Military Assistance and Advisory Group-Vietnam (USMAAGV). Its mission was to train the army of the newly created noncommunist government in the south, the Republic of Viet Nam.

In May 1964, USMAAGV was dissolved, its responsibilities and people absorbed into the United States Military Assistance Command, Vietnam (USMACV), which had been created in 1962. Its first commander was General Paul D. Harkins; his deputy was General William C. Westmoreland. The number of American military personnel assigned to Viet Nam began to mushroom. When John F. Kennedy was elected president in 1960 there were about nine hundred members of America's armed forces in Viet Nam. By the time of his 1963 death in Dallas, the number had grown to more than twenty-five thousand.

Then came the Tonkin Bay incident. On 2 August 1964, the USS *Maddox*, an electronically enhanced intelligence-gathering destroyer, acting as part of Operation De Soto,[1] was attacked by patrol torpedo boats of the northern communist government while operating in the Gulf of Tonkin. Two days later, when *Maddox* had been joined by a sister ship, the USS *C. Turner Joy*, the North Vietnamese boats allegedly launched a second attack against both. As a result and at the request of President Lyndon Johnson, on 7 August 1964, Congress passed the joint Tonkin Bay Resolution, giving Johnson the authority necessary to order the military to repel armed attacks against U.S. forces and to prevent further aggression. Johnson believed this resolution gave him a free hand to punish North Viet Nam for its attacks on the U.S. Navy. U.S. bombers swept across the Seventeenth Parallel, attacking patrol boat bases and oil storage depots.

The Vietnamese enemy now began to target American military personnel and bases. General Westmoreland, now commander of USMACV, asked for additional troops. On 8 March 1965, the first U.S. Marine combat units in Viet Nam arrived at Da Nang. The Army came close on their heels. The 173d Light Infantry Brigade (Airborne) was the first Army combat unit to reach Viet Nam, arriving In-Country on 7 May 1965. It was soon involved in combat operations.

---

[1]Operation De Soto was a U.S. program, using certain vessels of the Seventh Fleet equipped with electronic equipment, to photograph, map locations, and measure frequencies of coastal radar stations, in addition to monitoring shipping and Naval traffic along the coastline of the Democratic Republic of Viet Nam (the North). While commandos of the Republic of Viet Nam landed shore parties at various locations to harass radar installations, electronic intelligence (ELINT) ships recorded resulting electronic transmissions. The operation was authorized by President Johnson in late 1963.

It was augmented by a brigade of the 101st Airborne Division (Air Mobile). Other units followed. The military buildup, which eventually reached 550,000, had begun. The United States had taken over responsibility for conducting the war against the enemies of the Republic of Viet Nam.

This dramatic increase in the number of American military personnel serving in Viet Nam made it inevitable that, sooner or later, some would break one or another of the rules of the *Uniform Code of Military Justice* that bound them all. Most were young, lacking the maturity that comes with age. Temptations lay everywhere for these testosterone-laden men. Some felt empowered by their training and the weapons they carried and believed that normal rules of behavior no longer applied to them. In the early days, those who broke military regulations found themselves incarcerated at Pershing Field. Commanders of that facility included, among others, Captain Walter Shumway and Major Dale Groenenboom.

Then, in the summer of 1966, after operating only a few months, Pershing Field was closed down. Under the direction of Major Groenenboom, its prisoners and staff were relocated some thirty kilometers east of Saigon at the juncture of two rivers in the province of Long Binh. There the Army built a new facility. At Pershing Field the lock-up had been known simply as "The Stockade." The new confinement pen was not long in acquiring a more distinctive name. Its official name was the United States Army Vietnam Installation Stockade (USARVIS). GIs commonly referred to it as Long Binh Jail, or simply LBJ.

Tom Guidera, first commander of the 18th MP Brigade, tells how it began.

18TH MP BRIGADE COMMANDER TOM GUIDERA: "It was in mid-'66. The brigade was ordered to move to Long Binh. There was *nothin'* there. It was just a junction in the rivers. My 18th Brigade, its headquarters and two of its units, moved out there. We just set up camp. An Engineer brigade was assigned at the same time. It had the [necessary] earth-moving equipment and we proceeded to build a camp. We went to the Book [Army regulations] to see how it was done, and we built Long Binh Jail. We built a one-time light enclosure, moved prisoners in there, and we had them build their own stockade. They did the whole thing. It was pretty simple."

It may not have been as simple as Guidera remembered. Sergeant Marion Powers was one of the first MP guards to arrive at Long Binh.

GUARD POWERS: "About six months after I arrived we moved out to LBJ. Engineers had cleared out jungle with bulldozers back an eighth to a quarter mile. We were assigned to help build the stockade with prisoner labor. It was *miserable*—not compared to other units in the field, but we were used to tents over concrete slabs, footlockers, so our lives weren't too bad. But when we moved out there it was pallets on the ground. You put your bunk on the pallet and tried to arrange it in such fashion that it didn't fall through onto the ground. We set up our tents over the pallets. [At first] we used pallets for walk mats—no PSP [perforated steel planking]—to the restrooms and showers. They were minimal make-shift."

Completing the stockade took awhile. James Pederson recalled what USARVIS looked like when he arrived at Long Binh later in the year, perhaps September.

MP OFFICER JAMES PEDERSON: "[T]hey had at the time just a cyclone fence . . . and all the prisoners and cadre [staff] were living in tents. Being the new person, I was put in charge of some of the construction and built the disciplinary and administrative segregation cells, the chapel, etc., with prison labor. The 720th MP Battalion provided some stockade guards. By the time I went to Long Binh, they already had the lights completed, towers were built, outside double-apron cyclone fencing was all up. PSP [perforated steel planking] was put down and tents put up on it.

"There were three compounds. One held all the custody prisoners, minimum, medium, and maximum—all segregated basically by distance. No interior fences at the time. There was one compound where incoming prisoners were brought, and that's where our processing center was located. The cadre slept in two tents—enlisted in one, officers in the other. All tents had sandbag walls around them to keep grazing fire from entering them. A mess hall and the administrative building were completed by the time I got there. Like most units then, we used outhouses.

"Then, as we got materials, we boxed in tents with wooden flooring and wooden frames. Tent flaps raised during the day and dropped at night. [The buildings] met all the standards. We had engineering drawings for them. . . . We built the chapel. We found that if we took prisoners and invoked their pride, they could really do a good job—and they built a beautiful chapel."

In those early days, as guards and prisoners alike stared at the nearby jungle, all were aware that they were deep within troubled territory. Guidera remembered the orders he gave while the facility was under construction.

18TH MP BRIGADE COMMANDER TOM GUIDERA: "I put certain prisoners on guard at night. Anti-VC protection. Sentries. No one ran away because we were out in VC country."

Sam Mullin, an MP with the 557th, also remembered those early days.

GUARD MULLIN: "The jungle was right across the road from us and we had some unfriendly 'stuff' coming at us once in awhile. Finally the damn Engineers plowed the area and pushed the jungle back. Then the 720th [MP Battalion] deployed, probably in November 1966 . . . . Then beyond the 720th, the 89th Group set up and then headquarters of the 18th MP Brigade and then behind them the 18th MP CID [criminal investigation detachment] set up. We kept expanding and growing. The 24th MEDEVAC [medical evacuation] hospital was built kitty-corner to us and the next thing you know, Long Binh was rapidly becoming a very big city . . . , which pushed everything a mile away from the stockade. We had no immediate perimeter problem after that."

Mullin's memory, while good, was not exact. The 18th Military Police Brigade had two subordinate commands: the 8th Military Police Group and the 89th Military Police Group. The 8th MPG carried out criminal investigations. The 89th MPG had four MP battalions assigned to it: the 92nd, 95th, 716th, and 720th.[2]

---

[2] U.S. Army Military History Institute, Carlisle Barracks, Carlisle, PA, 13 November 1989.

The headquarters complex for USARV, including LBJ, grew so fantastically that, at a cost of more than 100 million dollars, it eventually occupied some twenty-five square miles, and housed more than fifty thousand soldiers. By mid-1967 about half of the Army personnel in Saigon relocated to Long Binh.[3]

The area expanded so much and so quickly that Long Binh Jail needed a street address: 10 Hall Road. A sign over the main gate of LBJ proclaimed: "We Welcome Command Failures." The sign was flanked by the symbol of the Military Police—crossed pistols.[4]

The confinement officer in charge of the move, Major Dale Groenenboom, had also headed the stockade when it was still at Pershing Field. Now, in the first days at the new location, he began to suffer from headaches. Before long they became debilitating. Seeking medical help, Groenenboom was soon diagnosed by military physicians as having a brain tumor. He was put on medical leave, evacuated home, and processed for retirement.

MP Sergeant Sam Mullin was one of those involved in transshipping prisoners from Pershing to Long Binh and in the construction of the new facility there.

GUARD MULLIN: "I went out to Long Binh [from Pershing] about nine times with groups of about thirty parolees. We helped the Engineers to unroll the fence line because we had to put up two sixteen-foot fences. Two eight-foot fences locked together, as well as sandbag five towers. We had Engineer cranes, and the guys wired them together. It took maybe three days to fence in the compound.

"While waiting for the DSEG [disciplinary segregation area] to be built, we used fourteen conex containers for DSEG. They were hell."

Sergeant Marion Powers talked further about those containers.

GUARD POWERS: "Maximum security [inmates] lived in conex boxes. Little slats were cut out to make bars. A cot, mosquito net, blanket, Bible, a can or bucket to use. Prisoners had a pair of boxer shorts, boots, that's all. The rest of their stuff was kept in a basket in a

[3]Carrol H. Dunn, *Base Development in South Vietnam, 1965–1970* (Washington, DC: Department of Army, 1972), pp. 77, 145.

[4]John Berry, *Those Gallant Men: On Trial in Vietnam* (Novato, CA: Presidio Press, 1984), p. 22.

locked area of a building, a warehouse storage area, so that when he got out his stuff would supposedly still be there. There were possibly fifteen boxes modified to be jail cells, with locks on the outside, guards stationed outside.

"Guards had a tin-roofed building with real low sides so they could stay in there and still see the prisoners. Every shift we'd take one or two of the prisoners to take a shower or whatever they needed or see a commander or something administratively. That's what the guards did. Take care of their needs. Escort them back and forth. Their toiletries were kept for them. They could use them when [they were] taken out [of a conex] box. A toothbrush could be sharpened off and turned into a knife. They could do their daily hygiene even in maximum."

GUARD MULLIN: "Once we got the 557th set up inside Compound One, we developed Compound Three. Compound Two was, of course, the admin[istration] section. It seemed like we filled that [inmate] general population in days. First we threw up tents. We had a couple of ammo dump explosions, and the prisoners went into a total panic. We had built one great big bomb shelter in one corner of Compound Three, but it was like bedlam for people to get into it."

Sergeant Powers added his recollection that the bunker was made of concrete, perhaps thirty to forty feet long and twenty feet wide.

GUARD POWERS: "[I]n case of attack there'd be some place to go."

It is no wonder the inmates panicked when Long Binh was attacked by mortars or satchel charges smuggled in and hidden by enemy sappers. Powers remembered one of those explosions.

GUARD POWERS: "There was an eleven-acre ammo dump nearby, within a stone's throw of our compound. It was arranged in such a way that there were pallets of ammunition, gasoline, oil. It was more like a supply dump. There was *everything* inside there. The 557th [MP Battalion] had personnel who made the rounds within the perimeter of that ammo dump in an armored jeep. Two guards. The driver and a gunner who manned a .50 caliber machine gun, going up and down the rows of pallets and supplies.

"About September or October 1966 some VC got inside and set

satchel charges. The first satchel charge went off when we were in bed, I suppose around ten o'clock, and it blew ammo into other pallets and then they would explode. A chain reaction. It sounded like they were right there at the end of our tent. We got the word to hit the bunker and we ran and got in it. We stayed in there for probably about three hours and it was constant explosions. Finally it was all-clear. We went back to our tents. There were shell casings, pieces of metal, fragments of everything that was in that dump over in our compound. Literally thrown into the sky. There were holes in the roofs of the tents and in the walls. . . . They never got the guys who set it off. They never found the guards in the jeep who were making the rounds. Pieces of the jeep, but no guys."

GUARD MULLIN: "[After that attack] I suggested to the provost marshal that we get the augur truck and the trench digger and dig slit trenches between each tent. Put the tents in frames and get rid of the rope so we won't have rope between each tent. So the prisoners boxed them in and put the tents on floors. . . . We finally got them settled down into that living environment."

GUARD POWERS: "[The new stockade had] four towers, one at each corner. . . . It was about a city block in depth and width. Later they added to it with more fencing and took in another block. Two city blocks of stockade. They added two more towers so ended up with six. . . . Our first living area—the tents in which we stayed—was in the last quadrant of the stockade they encompassed. [Prisoners] built hooches across the road from the stockade for us to live in. At first they were just tents and then prisoners built . . . concrete slab barracks with vented slats all the way around and then screened inside up to the top with tents over that—made it sort of like a house. Probably ten or twelve in a tent, so we had plenty of room for a cot, footlockers, wall lockers."

Outside were sidewalks formed out of two-by-four boards.

"[There was] an entrance at the corner of the stockade to bring prisoners in; a sally port and a guard station and a reception center—just tents—at the gate where they processed prisoners in. A clerk was there to type information on forms, an officer-of-the-day, a few officers in charge. They had their offices inside the wire but separate from the stockade."

GUARD MULLIN: "The mess hall was the first building we put up. The food was excellent. People came from all over Long Binh to make friends with an MP just so they could go in and have the prisoners' chow."

Sergeant Powers elaborated on the mess hall.

GUARD POWERS: "When we lived within the stockade area we ate with the prisoners. All the bread they baked had bugs in it because the wheat did. So they just went ahead and baked it. If you wanted bread, you picked the bugs out and ate it. Prison cooks prepared the food. The mess hall was divided down the middle, and inmates ate on one side and administrative personnel, guards, and the 557th MP personnel ate on the other side."

GUARD MULLIN: "I designed the chapel. Supervised its erection. They wouldn't let me put a crucifix on the roof so I put one on the door. A screen door with sun rays. We put louvered sides on it, screened it in so there were no bugs, no flies, no gnats when you went in for a service. The prisoners enjoyed working on it. The prisoners tried to put a secret trap door in the confessional, and I caught two of them up on the ceiling on a lunch break. I caught one huge black inmate with one pretty little white boy—and they both went into DSEG. Fourteen days for disobeying an NCO. I never wrote them up for fucking with each other.

"When the DSEG unit was finally completed it was magnificent. When you got in there you never saw the outside. Hot as a bastard! The heat radiated off that hot tin roof. About 135° inside. Conexes were just as hot. Inmates stayed in their underwear. Too hot to wear clothes. Course we had them boxed in with concertina wire."

Inmate Private Vernon Shippee was one of those on construction.

INMATE SHIPPEE: "I helped build LBJ. It was in the middle of an MP compound. We filled sandbags. We built wooden floors for GP [general purpose] tents. They also had conex boxes. . . . When the new camp first opened, we ate in the MP mess hall, so everybody ate the same basic food."

When completed, the stockade area was roughly the size of two square city blocks. It was constructed to house between 550 and 575 inmates. Prisoners' quarters were tents with wooden floors. The administration buildings were located in the central compound, on each side of which was another compound in which prisoners were kept. Those two prisoner compounds were divided into three areas: minimum—where prisoners could be escorted without an armed guard; medium—where prisoners needed an armed guard escort; maximum—where prisoners were primarily kept caged and could not leave the compound.

Daily routine consisted of reveille at 5 A.M., chow, then prisoners would be assigned work details at 6 A.M. Much of the work required was on a par with stateside prisons where inmates made license plates. Prisoners worked until noon, returned to the stockade for lunch, then went back to their work assignments until 4 P.M. They had free time between the end of their work details and the evening meal. Lights out at night came between 9 and 10 P.M.

Life at the newly constructed facility got under way. Administration personnel processed paperwork. Guards watched inmates. Prisoners, for various reasons, seethed. It did not take long for inmate resentment to bubble over. The first sign of prisoner unrest became evident in late December 1966. MP Sergeant Marion Powers told how a riot broke out at that time.

GUARD POWERS: "I wasn't on duty that night. There were two minimum security compounds within the original stockade and a maximum security enclosure where they kept prisoners waiting to be sent [back] to [serve sentences at the disciplinary barracks at] Leavenworth. The majority of prisoners were black.

"There was a full complement of MPs because there had been racial tensions during the day. . . . I was in the compound and got called out. . . . We put on our riot gear and had weapons, but no bullets, and bayonets attached [to our rifles] with the scabbard on them. That was in case the thing escalated to the point that our lives would be in danger.

"I remember being in a wedge formation . . . second from the point. We were going into one of the fenced-off minimum security areas . . . . We were going in . . . and a black guy ran out with a stick in his hand. He took a swipe at this point man and the point man butted him with his rifle and broke his jaw. There were several others hurt during that riot. They were molesting guards or hurting another prisoner. That lasted probably no more than two hours. Not a whole lot of riot left in them after a few got hurt. I think the riot was quelled so quickly because tear gas takes the fight out of you."

# CHAPTER THREE

# LIFE INSIDE

By late 1966 LBJ took on the appearance it would keep for the next eighteen months. Cyclone fences and concertina wire on the perimeter. Lights on tall poles to illuminate the area at night. Guard towers at regular intervals manned by watchful men. An acceptable mess hall. An administration building. A chapel. Three compounds: Minimum, medium, and maximum security. Inmates facing pretrial confinement lived in Compound Three. Post-trial confinement for those waiting dispatch back to the United States was Compound One. Compound Two held the administration building, the mess hall, the chapel. Regular inmates slept in wooden boxes or on cots in tents with floors. Maximum security consisted of a set of conex boxes in double rows reworked into cells, protected from the sun by an overhead tarpaulin. It was known as Silver City. Troublemakers were housed there.

MP Major Norwood Jackson, executive officer under Lieutenant Colonel George Deringer, commented on how problem prisoners were treated in Silver City.

MAJOR JACKSON: "We did what was necessary and authorized at LBJ in terms of lock-ins. When a guy acted up he needed to be punished. . . . We didn't have areas for special treatment [when he was there 4 July 1967–4 July 1968]. . . . We didn't have standard cell blocks. We finally built some but didn't have them initially. . . . We built everything from the ground up. . . . When guys couldn't adjust, we put them in these conex containers. . . . The conex containers became a handy tool when they were available. . . . It didn't take long in there when it was 110° in the shade. . . . It didn't take a lot of time in one to get religion. They were metal boxes, and that sun on a hot tin roof helped people get the message pretty quick. The boxes established a stigma; it was a degrading experience whether they were comfortable or not. They became a symbol of something that probably did not exist as severely as people thought. Initially, though, when they sat in the sun, they were cruel containers. . . . That *was* kind of a medieval use of those conexes."

Silver City had a bad reputation among the prisoners. Many reported how hot the area was, how confining the cells in which they were placed. Some inmates believed it was known as Silver City because of the color of the canvas hung on the nearby fences. They were wrong. It was perhaps described best by Lieutenant Colonel Paul Grossheim, confinement officer from July 1970 to July 1971.

LIEUTENANT COLONEL GROSSHEIM: "The canvas round the outside had nothing to do with Silver City. That was for people walking down the public street right outside the fence [to keep them] from talking to inmates or inmates to them. It was felt there were a lot of vials of heroin that could be thrown over the fence to an inmate inside. If canvas was up, the inmate couldn't effectively set up a time and location on the perimeter to receive vials.

"Silver City was an area filled with conex containers. Their fronts were cut open and bars put along the front and a door. The corners were cut so air could flow inside. These were placed in rows similar to cell blocks [with perhaps] twelve or twenty-four in a line and four different aisles. They were all painted silver and over the top there was a tin-roofed building with support columns. A pole building. Corrugated metal roof with nothing on the sides. That [also] was painted silver. The top reflected the sun's heat. Then there was a space of eight or ten feet between that top and the conexes. That allowed air to circulate. . . . Often times it was one of the coolest areas you could have.

"Imagine what you could do if you wanted . . . . Lock an inmate up in a conex container out in the sun and paint it black!! But in Silver City, if it were 110° outside, I can guarantee it would never be over 110° inside the conex. If there was a breeze, it was . . . comfortable . . . .

The problem with them is that they were probably no more than 6′2″ high. Ten feet by ten feet was adequate room as far as space inside goes but not enough headroom."

Another maximum security area was added later. Eight cells constructed of two-by-eight boards set on a concrete slab, clustered together with a common wall down the middle. Each cell had a slot cut out of the door large enough to slide food trays through.

Inmates not confined in maximum or disciplinary segregation had an easier time of it. Major Wesley Vaughan Geary, a former chaplain, recalled life at LBJ as he saw it.

CHAPLAIN GEARY: "It was a typical stockade. A lot of the guys worked up at the hospital and around there outside the wire. In fact, they enjoyed it. That was my concern. They'd rather be in the stockade than out in the field. . . . The duty was good and people weren't getting shot at."

Due to circumstances beyond the control of the authorities in charge of LBJ, the prisoner population grew rapidly. Tom Guidera, founding 18th MP Brigade commander, described how that happened.

18TH MP BRIGADE COMMANDER TOM GUIDERA: "[A]ll the divisions would evacuate their general prisoners to us and we held them until shipment back to CONUS [continental United States]. Short-timers could return to their units after serving their time. A lot of inmates were hard-cases. We had a lot of confinement cells that we used for the bad-news guys in there. They were in for violent crimes. . . . Those inmates didn't get in there by accident.

"Don't believe these guys when they talk to you. They weren't in there because they were good soldiers. They were in there because they were *thugs*. They committed crimes against the population, against their own units. We had guys in there who, for example, shot and killed Vietnamese on a whim. Bad-news guys, but we treated them according to the Book."

Specialist Fourth Class Mike Doherty, a computation clerk on the stockade staff, told how the Book worked for new arrivals: "In-processing was simple. We never knew when we would get somebody new. They'd come in with one or two guards. They were strip-searched, looking in all their cavities for contraband."

LBJ had a procedure for everything, including one that involved those who brought prisoners to the stockade, visiting lawyers from the Judge Advocate General staff who represented inmates, officers of various commands who might have occasion to enter the compound, everyone. Officers often carried only a pistol sidearm. One who visited regularly has noted that each time he passed through the gate, the ritual was the same: "[R]emove pistol from holster, dry fire into red bucket, check in the cleared weapon. Then the briefcase inspection: flash the open valise at the bored specialist."[1]

One of those responsible for such regulations was confinement officer Lieutenant Colonel George Deringer, who held his position from July 1967 to July 1968. He came to LBJ as an experienced MP officer. He had previously served at the Fort Bragg, North Carolina, stockade for the XVIII Airborne Corps, on special assignment from the 82nd Airborne MP Company. He had attended the MP Confinement School and the Security School at Fort Gordon, Georgia.

LIEUTENANT COLONEL DERINGER: "The adopted motto which I established after arrival was FIRM BUT FAIR. . . . The stockade functioned pretty much (as near as possible) to the dictates of established doctrine set down by Army regulations. Guiding manuals regarding discipline and overall handling of confinees were adhered to. From basic introductory briefings on entry as a prisoner to release on competent orders from the prisoner's unit, the stockade functioned 'according to the book.'

"Prisoners were fed, clothed, [and] supplied basic needs for personal comfort, hygienically as well as items for protection from the elements. . . . Each prisoner on entry was seen by a social worker—categorized, processed and admitted. Entries and releases occured practically daily. Units delivered and units picked up.

"At the onset of my arrival—as best I recall—there were somewhere around two or three hundred prisoners. A year later that figure had doubled."

Inmate Private James B. Vaughan, who served forty-two days at LBJ in pretrial confinement, remembered his arrival.

---

[1]Berry, *Those Gallant Men*, p. 22.

INMATE VAUGHAN: "They took me in and gave me the regular booking procedure—strip naked, balls lift, balls left, balls right, look up your butt hole, look in your arm pits, in your mouth, between your fingers, in your hair, behind your ears—the whole thing."

SPECIALIST FOURTH CLASS DOHERTY: "We'd check their gear for contraband, dope, and weapons. . . . They'd get a shower and a brush hair cut."

Vaughan remembered his hair.

INMATE VAUGHAN: "[My hair] was so long it was incredible. . . . I stood in front of the mirror [at the barbershop] and started combing out my hair. This young shavetail lieutenant said 'Hurry up, get your ass in the chair, you piece of shit'. . . . A captain that was with him told him to shut up and let the man have his peace.

"It might take one or two hours to run a guy through the process. . . . If a guy was good and kept his nose clean, he did okay. After he got there he might work for two or three weeks at Big Red [filling sandbags] and then make his way up to parolee. . . . Then he could go outside to Long Binh installation to work at odds and ends that needed doing—painting, cleaning, and so forth. They wore regular fatigues with no rank and with yellow stripes on their sleeves and trouser legs. Sometimes they were escorted, but some were allowed to walk back and forth unescorted. They had to be back inside by the dinner curfew. . . . He'd get five days a month off the length of his sentence for good behavior."

INMATE PRIVATE GERALD STOVALL: "Procedures going in? They gave us the rules and regulations, some toiletries, told us what area we would be assigned to . . . . I was assigned to medium side, the largest side where most everybody was at. From there to minimum, which meant you are allowed to work outside the compound."

Lieutenant Colonel Deringer seems to have been responsible for insisting on more control of prisoners' waking hours. Prior to his arrival it may have been the case that inmates spent most days in their respective compound yards, talking, milling about, taking the sun, and generally relaxing. Deringer put a stop to that.

LIEUTENANT COLONEL DERINGER: "Inside the stockade we introduced a work area nicknamed 'Big Red.' It was where sand would be trucked in and prisoners detailed to fill sandbags. The 'Big Red' referred to the sun above. It was a hot place to work but served a vital purpose. Units were in dire need of sandbags. Trucks, as well as 'choppers,' would haul the bags away as fast as we could fill them. The choppers would fly in and take them out in big nets on which we put the filled bags. There were more demands than could be met. As best I recall, a million had been filled during my tenure. I like to think many bullets were stopped by those sandbags. . . . There's a possible hitch in my memory but I seem to recall one prisoner allowing himself to be covered with sandbags on an outgoing flat bed [truck]. Whether he was asphyxiated or nearly died before discovery I can't say for sure. We tightened our security and went on from there. The 'Big Red' lived on. I can't tell you how many inspectors, unit commanders, sergeant majors, etc., viewed that operation. Nothing but thanks came from their mouths. [For those who labored there] adequate rest, water, and constant surveillance were the standards. It worked!"

MP Major Norwood Jackson agreed with his commander's assessment of the value of work details.

MAJOR JACKSON: "We did get them to work feverishly when they thought they were doing something that contributed to the mission. We developed a work program there. We had an area we called Big Red. We used to break up laterite—a hard, red clay—there and use it to fill sandbags. We started out working them in this yard as a punishment and it rolled over to be a positive contribution to the war effort. We filled sandbags and flew them to the Delta and throughout the war zone as a contribution and these guys would get in that yard and work like Trojans just to get that mission accomplished. The heat problem was bad, so I used to give them a quota—fill so many bags and we'll knock off for the day. I put up a sign: "You're Now Entering Big Red." When we got that program structured so they knew what they had to do, there was no problem getting them to work and they worked hard getting that job accomplished."

MP OFFICER JAMES PEDERSON: "Engineers would bring dirt into the compound with dump trucks and we'd assign inmates to fill sandbags. We did that for a couple of reasons: one, it was helping all other units including those they came from . . . and second, it was something to do rather than just have them sit on their hands."

MAJOR JACKSON: "I [also] had a trustee policy. It worked very well. I identified jobs for trustees to do in ways that didn't conflict with dealing with other inmates. Otherwise they're viewed as finks or rats. We identified guys with some skills who wanted to work and those who didn't. . . . We had trustees who ran the kitchen, who did the work around the kitchen, those who had specific jobs in Big Red, those who could do mechanical work. We used them in that way. Before long I had a working force that begged to work.

"[We had parolees as well who] could go outside the wire and work in areas where the troops lived. They did cleaning in company areas instead of the guys working on the line. Worked in the orderly room or in the motor pool. They began to feel responsible for something, and we had no problem with that program.

"We housed them together, fed them together, and they were confined to a particular area. Housing had to be clean, rules followed, or everybody got punished. . . . They learned to clean, and to keep themselves clean, to fall out in uniform like they was a regular outfit. . . . We don't feed them one thing and the staff another. Make it a point to feed your people where they can see the food is the same. Make it a point also that when you give out discipline, give it out for a reason to someone who genuinely needs to be disciplined. Do that in a uniform way. That worked for me. . . . [S]et a uniform standard of treatment for everybody as well as uniform discipline treatment. They saw we generally attended to their needs. Hygiene, food, and clothing. Then there's no reason for them to fight you. You know, we don't solicit business!"

Although officers may have been proud of implementing this program, prisoners viewed it differently.

INMATE VAUGHAN: "[Y]our first detail in medium security was Big Red. All you did was to fill fifty [sandbags] in the morning—you and your partner—he had to hold fifty for you and you had to hold fifty for him in the morning and the same thing in the afternoon. That was cruel and unusual punishment as far as I'm concerned and you can quote me on that."

INMATE PRIVATE RUDOLPH GRAY: "We worked sometimes in Big Red. . . . It was red clay. . . . After working there, no matter what color you were when you went in, everybody looked alike coming out."

INMATE STOVALL: "Big Red was just awful. You had this red dirt and had to fill all these sandbags with the guards standing on top of you calling all the shots. I can't see anybody saying that's fun. Nobody volunteered. Guys were constantly going on sick call to get a [medical] profile to keep from going to Big Red. I don't think many of the guys you'll come across will have many good things to say about . . . Big Red."

If prisoners didn't like working at Big Red, guards could always find something else for them to do. Some of the other jobs were not much more pleasant.

GUARD MULLIN: "If an inmate was a real pain in the ass, I'd let him drive a Cadillac all day. We had the smoothest ground inside that compound that there was in all Viet Nam. We had that Cadillac operating almost eighteen hours a day, and they became expert drivers."

SOCIAL WORKER WAYNE PRICE: "The 'Cadillac' was a two-man broom used to sweep the dirt."

INMATE VAUGHAN: "After about five days of Big Red, they made me a street sweeper and I had to start at the big gate—the start of the medium compound and it went all the way down past the mess hall, the offices on one side and the medium compound on the other—and I had to sweep with one of those great big straw brooms. Me and another guy had to sweep that son of a bitch down and some asshole will come along and say, 'I saw some dust up in the gutter. Go back to the gate and sweep it again.' So you may end up sweeping that thing four times one morning and six times one afternoon. That was about the biggest abuse. They were badgering and baiting me to screw up and send me back to max."

SOCIAL WORKER PRICE: "Work details were about half a dozen inmates with about two guard escorts. Guards carried mostly shotguns, some [carried] .45s."

INMATE PRIVATE ROBERT JACKSON: "I got assigned to help clean up the personal property room and type cards concerning property and status."

INMATE GRAY: "I burnt shit, cleaned up, policed the area. . . . I was to do hard labor; that was picking up cigarette butts.

"LBJ was not a scary place [for those who were not in disciplinary segregation]; it was not as bad as it seemed. . . . In 1967 there were no permanent buildings, just tents. The tents were maybe ten feet apart. Each tent held fifteen to twenty guys. Each inmate had a cot, a footlocker. We had a mosquito net over our bunks. The tents had no sides, just a top and a wooden floor. . . A latrine was maybe ten yards away and we had to empty it by burning the shit. . . . We'd get up, exercise, do calisthenics every morning, eat breakfast, police the area twice a day. We took turns cuttin' hair. I barbered a lot. Some just would sit and sing, talk about home life, what they'd do when they got back in the States. Some would holler through the fence to passersby: WACS, nurses, friends, associates. They had a TV in the OR [orderly room]. We had close-order drills where we put our own steps into rhythms. No weapons to carry so used sticks instead. We sang. Talked about life, what they do in their hometown, get to know others fairly well. . . . We got regular GI food. Sometimes we had some real tough red meat—we thought it was water buffalo, but the cooks called it veal. It was no veal. . . . We had church every Sunday. I was a firm believer. . . . Mail call every day. . . . That's about it. It really wasn't bad. . . . The baddest part is when you're in, you think about life in general, period. Home, friends you can't see.

"The attitude of the guards all depends if you were a tough guy. A guy who thinks he's bad, who has no humor, who wants to whip up on everyone, jungle fatigue. . . . They *did* have a sweat box for guys who got out of hand. It was a one-man sized bunker. . . . One person who'd stay all crunched up. They might give you a day.

"Sometimes there was a water shortage. They had to ration drinking water. Hard to bathe except during monsoons. You smelled. Others did too. We'd stand in the rain with a cloth. Best time was monsoon times."

INMATE VAUGHAN: "Mainly during the day when I was in maximum security I went outside and pulled off my shirt and shot baskets. I played basketball. That's what the trustees did. Sit out there in 100–120° weather and shoot baskets."

INMATE PRIVATE CHARLES KRIES: "I worked at Big Red. At first I filled sandbags and then made concrete blocks. Then I got in the mess hall. Worked scullery. Then became night cook and then night baker. . . . I remember when a bunch of us . . . drank some apple jack, which we had made from dehydrated apples. . . . We all got drunk and were listening to music, having a good time when we got caught by the sergeant in charge. Lucky for us he just laughed and then dumped the rest of it down the drain."

18TH MP BRIGADE COMMANDER TOM GUIDERA: "[Inmates] might tell you hard luck stories of bad treatment, but did they also tell you they had every Sunday off? They played games while soldiers were pulling duty that Sunday. . . . I couldn't get rid of them fast enough. . . . And it grew and grew, and [we] wound up with about four hundred people in it by the time I left. We just couldn't get their sentences approved [fast enough] and the men evacuated to the United States."

Guidera's four hundred was just a start. The American military presence was growing rapidly, and the number of miscreants increased proportionally. A few months after his departure the number of inmates approached one thousand men. The facility, built to house a much smaller number of prisoners, became hopelessly overcrowded. And those additional confinees caused problems other than simple overcrowding.

Although the Military Police Corps (MPC) was small in size, its personnel carried out numerous duties throughout the U.S. Army. Small groups of MPs were assigned to larger Army units to provide each with a police presence. These MPs directed traffic and investigated vehicular accidents. They served as the "highway patrol" of the military, ticketing speeders. They stood at the entrances to military bases controlling who could and could not enter and checking identification. They were responsible for processing prisoners of war. They provided rear area security for combat units. They investigated crimes against persons and property. They manned all the stockades within the Army, worldwide.

Within the Corps, individual members were also assigned diverse tasks. After their training perhaps a majority functioned as police, but not all. Some served as clerks. Some handed out supplies. Some planned operations. A few served as security personnel for important officers. All enlisted personnel who entered the Corps received the same fundamental training culminating in the award of a 95-B military occupation specialty (MOS).

In earlier days, however, those MPs whose performance was substandard in some way were often assigned to watch over stockade prisoners. They were called "prisoner chasers." Authorities believed that these jobs required few skills. Consequently, the quality and training of many MPs assigned to stockades was not high. Within this assignment, the lowest rung on the ladder was always the job of watching prisoner work details and escorting inmates between facilities.

Given these circumstances, in the early days of LBJ the Corps was not really prepared to staff a stockade the size of LBJ with competent and properly trained guards. Military authority within the Corps assigned guards to the stockade who had little or no professional training as confinement facility specialists, and the Corps at the time actually had no correctional educational training programs. Height, weight, and toughness seemed to be the primary qualifications for such a job. Once in charge of prisoners, these MPs imposed a rigid and exacting set of disciplinary standards and demanded that prisoners obey them at all times. Infractions brought immediate, sometimes physical, punishment. Compounding these problems, USARV Headquarters at Long Binh sometimes sent individuals from other branches of the Army with no MP training at all to work at the stockade.

It was not until the middle years of the Viet Nam conflict that Corps authorities came to understand that working with prisoners required special training. They finally authorized a new MOS, a 95-C "Confinement Specialist," and set up courses at the MP School at Fort Gordon, Georgia, to train MPs in this area. Many graduates went to Viet Nam, assigned to LBJ.

MP OFFICER JAMES PEDERSON: "Assigning MPs as guards to punish them was a 1950s concept. Some remnants still existed in the '60s. I was at Fort Lewis in the '60s, and some of the MPs there [still] warned their subordinates: 'If you goof up, you're going to the stockade as a prisoner chaser.'

"I was involved later in establishing the 95-Charley [MOS] training program at the MP School at Fort Gordon in the late 1960s. Part of the program was based on my experiences at USARVIS. . . . The professional training program . . . progressed quite well. Those [with that new MOS] were put [to work] in the stockade. We rotated them around in different assignments so they didn't get stale. . . . Our training taught that you never used a closed fist or kicked anybody."

Captain William Hart, who later rose to the rank of full colonel and who served as Commandant at the Disciplinary Barracks at Fort Leavenworth, described the problems involved in using MPs who did not have adequate training.

WILLIAM HART: "[Early on] there were a lot of problems [with guards]. It was very difficult. We were undermanned and staffed by the wrong people. At that time, [higher headquarters] chose people for the stockade by who was available. . . . So a lot of guys they sent were truck drivers, cooks, infantrymen, and they were sent to the 54th MP Company, to work in the stockade—people who had no desire or aptitude to work in corrections. The results were disastrous."

MP officer James Pederson served two tours in Viet Nam, one in 1966–1967 and one in 1970–1971. During the latter tour he spent a few days in July 1971 as temporary confinement officer at LBJ. He spoke of his first tour in the early days of USARVIS.

JAMES PEDERSON: "We did use guards from the 720th Battalion as tower guards and in other noncritical areas. . . . MP guards were assigned out of the 720th. . . . We formed them up and gave them specific duties. A number of them were rotated in and out and we never let them have that much close contact with the prisoners. We put them on the gates to search vehicles as they came in or in towers with specific written instructions on their duties. . . . Those people never really got inside. . . . I think it was the 71st MP Detachment which processed people in and provided guards and compound officers.

"The training of our people improved a great deal in those early days. Military confinement went from taking MPs who were misbehaving and putting them in the stockade as guards as *their* punishment, to a very professionally trained group of people."

Major Norwood Jackson, executive officer under Lieutenant Colonel George Deringer, remembered his year of service at LBJ.

MAJOR JACKSON: "There's a level of respect due everybody. Some guards couldn't take what they dished out. I don't mean for the guards to be pussies, but to be firm but fair. Those who did their job objectively contributed to the whole program, but those who felt they were Jesus Christ after they put on that badge, I couldn't tolerate and got rid of them. I'm a hands-on operator. I'm not in the office but out there looking at them. I got to know inmates well.

"When I accepted the job they gave me a pretty free hand in getting some staff together. I got together some guys I knew; some were up in the combat zone; those I had known when I played football with them; some sergeants through lieutenants I knew. About a third of my staff were 95-C [confinement specialists]. . . . Initially most were just MP 95-Bravos. We didn't even have an abundance of those available, so used soldiers from nearby companies whose names came up on duty rosters. We had to do our own training of [those] 11-Bushes [actually 11-Bravos; "bush" was a soldier's way of saying where they spent most of their time]. Once we gave them some hands-on, some on-the-job training, they did pretty well, as long as the structure was there and we did the job of close supervision. We taught them how to deal with men, how to respect men regardless of who they were. We pretty much ran a straightforward, honest program. We didn't allow people to abuse people, but we dealt with them in a pretty stern way."

Chaplain (Major) Ralph Ludwig served in Viet Nam from June 1971 to March 1972. He was stationed at Da Nang, not LBJ, and had no firsthand experience with USARVIS. He was, however, familiar with a large Marine stockade in Da Nang that was eventually merged administratively with USARVIS. He seems not to have thought very highly of the guards there.

CHAPLAIN LUDWIG: "I visited LBJ one time and didn't go inside the gate. . . . [At Da Nang] guards treated prisoners like shit . . . . They didn't want to be there either. Some felt [inmates] were a disgrace to the . . . uniform."

MP Sergeant Sam Mullin described how he reacted when faced with a recalcitrant inmate.

GUARD MULLIN: "I'll handcuff [a troublemaker] and drag his ass down and throw him into a conex container and I'm going to keep that sonofabitch on the driest fourteen-day diet I can get away with."

Major Norwood Jackson was asked whether guards sometimes got out of hand in their treatment of inmates.

MAJOR JACKSON: "Never. Never."

MP Lieutenant Colonel Eugene Murdock had a different view. He remembered one of his guards.

LIEUTENANT COLONEL MURDOCK: "[One sergeant] would get out there and his goddamn eyes would get fire in them. He'd just look at them. Fact is, you got to watch guys like him. They'll get out there and get physical with them."

GUARD POWERS: "I thought prisoners at the first compound [Pershing] were treated fairly. There were no beatings. They were just soldiers who had gotten in trouble and were being detained. They were fed, clothed, they went on work details. [At LBJ] we started getting in maximum security prisoners who were more mean. We had roving guards walking the compound to keep prisoners from getting into the bunker and smoking their dope and fucking each other; go into the showers and see they weren't hiding out there; keep them from getting in fights and hurting one another. A lot seemed mentally unbalanced, what we now call PTSD [post-traumatic stress disorder]. They seemed to be the dregs of the units we covered. A lot were racially biased. I don't know how many times I've been called 'honky.'"

SOCIAL WORKER PRICE: "Guards patrolled security in twos. In maximum security they messed with prisoners a little, maybe being slow in responding to requests or not letting them out to go to the latrine. But nothing serious. . . . I have seen them hog-tie a guy with leg irons and handcuffs and chain him to the wall in a conex box. [H]e was creating some kind of behavioral problem . . . so he laid on the floor on his back and side with his legs and hands chained to the wall above him."

INMATE PRIVATE TERRY SMOOT: "I always had the feeling that the MPs, when they let me out to go to the bathroom, were just waiting for me to try to jump over the fence so they could shoot me. But I never had much problem with the guards. They were pretty tough guys and stood up straight."

LIEUTENANT COLONEL GEORGE DERINGER: "It was a tough job for each and every man at the LBJ. The prisoner population [3 July 1967–4 July 1968] was—almost to a man—composed of not first- or second-time offenders. These prisoners were sent from their units generally after they had been in trouble several times but retained at their respective combat locations. I suppose their commanding officers were reluctant to take these men out of combat to circumvent malingerers. But—of course—it gets to the point where unit integrity is endangered, thus necessitating confinement. . . . AWOL, illegal substances, assaults perhaps made up the bulk of offenses.

"Guards were well qualified, most who had previous confinement experience. This was a high-priority requirement. . . . [My executive officer] Major Norwood Jackson was highly instrumental in maintaining overall discipline within the LBJ. Without him my job would have been immensely more difficult."

The personalities and conduct of prisoners ranged across the spectrum of human behavior. Some were easy to work with and caused no problems. Others occasionally objected to their treatment or what they saw going on around them. Some, perhaps a great number, were incorrigible discipline-busters, hating the guards, the stockade, the system, their fellow prisoners, and the circumstances of their own lives.

CONFINEMENT OFFICER LIEUTENANT COLONEL WILLIE L. JONES: "Many of the men in the stockade there . . . were the real hardened characters, and nothing could have straightened them out. . . . I would probably have said they're going to wind up in jail again in civilian life. . . . But many of them were just kids. Probably the majority went straight once they got out. . . . We think of the thousands of these youngsters for whom it was a simple matter of AWOL. . . . [T]hat's enough to get you a month in the stockade. . . . They were just kids, real kids, and many of them were not even on drugs . . . . A great many of them were just frightened, confused. What do you do when you're just seventeen or eighteen years old?"

One former inmate witness who requested anonymity explained his change of heart while in LBJ. "I stole. I was guilty. I paid for it. I never stole again." Perhaps he and others like him were the ones Norwood Jackson had in mind.

MAJOR JACKSON: "Most of the kids in there were scared and in there for every kind of crime you can think of. Scared kids in a war zone are tough to work with. They reacted to pressures in a negative way.

"I saw kids come in . . . after having been in the field. . . . They'd . . . go to one of these whorehouses. Next thing they knew they was arrested by the MPs. Nobody [from their units] backed them. So we had to try to restore some self-respect in them; that they do make a contribution and not that they're there to be screwed. We communicated better in there than they did in the[ir] outfits."

SOCIAL WORKER GLORIA BERMAN: "Young boys—seventeen, eighteen, nineteen—went there at a time when people dream of doing important things with their lives: building, conquering disease, making real contributions. It's a special time for all of us to dream, and they did too. One of the men in my [PTSD] group said once: 'We all went there to find our manhood.' That's true! And at such a time they were trained to be soldiers and cause death and destruction. It's such a crucial time in a person's life. Some of them acted out forces inside them and were punished. Sometimes they did something irregular and were punished for it by the military courts-martial system. Or they did something today that was okay yesterday, and they also ended up in places like LBJ. It was a travesty!"

Not all those incarcerated at LBJ were in the situation described above. Some were, in fact, violent, disturbed criminals. A guard at the Marine stockade at Da Nang who wished to remain anonymous told of "one man [who] got to Viet Nam in 1967 . . . *never* wanted to leave. He was a bad hombre . . . . scary; had killed seven Marines: his gunnery sergeant, the first sergeant, the company commander, the mess sergeant, and some bystanders. . . . One day I saw a six- or eight-inch snake—a bamboo viper—crawl out of some vines and dart across an open stretch. . . . The killer picked it up, twirled it around his head. He had a long fingernail on his thumb. He inserted it in the snake's anus, split it open and ate it raw."

A Judge Advocate General officer, a lawyer, worked with inmates at LBJ on many occasions when he was a young man serving his year in Viet Nam. Captain Ben Yudesis suggested, too, that you could not generalize about prisoners.

CAPTAIN YUDESIS: "What kind of prisoners? We saw a variety. I was in private practice before coming into the service, both as a city prosecutor plus a criminal practice attorney in state and federal court. You saw all categories at LBJ. You saw what I would consider absolute cold-blooded killers with no redeeming social values, drug addicts, some who were situational drug addicts who just couldn't stand the strain there.

"We had some guys who were fairly decent in there. For some reason or another they had just stepped on it and ended up in jail. We had some guys—not only my opinion but that of others as well—who were absolutely straight prisoners. Never had any problems with them. . . . They were problems [in their units], but inside the facility . . . with institutional atmosphere and discipline where rules were clear, they were good soldiers. . . . An example was the Son Tay raid [an unsuccessful, late 1970 mission to rescue American POWs held near Ha Noi in North Viet Nam]. We must have had seventy-five volunteers who came and said if they do it again, we volunteer to go with them. Things like that stirred up the inmates.

"Some of those prisoners with no redeeming social value were eighteen- or nineteen-year-old boys; some a little older. But they might well have been exactly the same had they never come in the service. . . . I would guess that maybe 75 percent of the inmates would have been in trouble with the law had they never come into the service.

"A lot of the guys we had in there were jailed for drug offenses, black marketeering, AWOL, and serious crimes of violence. . . . We had murderers, people who assaulted superiors or fragged them, robbery, field refusals. . . . We ended with six [Air Force] security police dog handlers who suddenly decided they were conscientious objectors. . . . We had the SEAL team, including the OIC [officer-in-charge] who were smuggling narcotics back to the States in their classified equipment. . . . The team chief was in Australia on R & R when they picked him up and brought him in along with two others. They had some of the biggest Marine officers guarding him I've ever seen in my life. [T]hey were [eventually] transported back [to the continental United States] on separate planes, each one a sole passenger. Not all [such] transports were for the DB [disciplinary barracks at Fort Leavenworth]. Short-term prisoners—those whose enlistment would expire in six months—were sent to the confinement facility closest to their home."

MP OFFICER JAMES PEDERSON: "We had quite a few prisoners in for serious crimes: murder, assault . . . . One man, an Air Force NCO, had murdered five Vietnamese. He was drunk one night and went out to the end of the airfield where Vietnamese were picking up brass [ammunition] casings caused by pilots target practicing or getting rid of ammo before they landed. . . . He shot five of those people.

"Not as many [inmates] were there [for drug convictions] as when I went back the second time. . . . I wasn't surprised. I could see many coming back from Viet Nam [when I served in CONUS between Viet Nam tours] who were that way. The first time there were people on drugs . . . but not nearly like I saw the second time."

CONFINEMENT OFFICER LIEUTENANT COLONEL BILL KEYES: "You really can't do anything with 15 percent of the people who go into a stockade, and society never will. They're sociopathic personalities. Another 15 percent, the minute they committed the offense, their consciences started hurting them so bad they were punished beyond what anybody in the stockade could do to them anyway. That other 70 percent fall somewhere in between. As far as rehabilitation, we should see that [inmates] get educated, more literate, [show them] how families are supposed to operate, how citizens are supposed to operate. Then we need to get down on our knees and pray it takes."

Inmates complained loudly and long about the brutality visited on them while they were confined at LBJ. Did that brutality really occur? Not according to some, although they tended to be staff, not inmates.

LIEUTENANT COLONEL DERINGER: "The LBJ was not isolated in any way from the interests of COs [commanding officers], South Vietnamese officials (Army), visiting stateside officials (MPC, etc). I was in a constant state of readiness to tour-brief and explain the LBJ operation. . . . My charts were updated daily with such breakdowns as total number of prisoners, what units, offenses, custody breakdowns, including the real incalcitrants in disciplinary segregation. These were the truly hard-core guys who simply would not adhere to discipline. They caused 95 percent of our problems.

"Brigadier General Gustafson was a *very frequent* inspector of the facility. Getting a call of a 7 A.M. visit was not uncommon. He insisted on a daily briefing either by phone or an on-site visit. . . . [I]t kept everyone on his toes. The doctors for daily or semi-daily visits of prisoners in solitary was an absolute necessity (along with daily sick-call). No prisoner died or became seriously ill due to lack of medical attention. Doctors were available around the clock. The IG's presence was near daily. Prisoners had the right to complain—and did frequently. The IG would see them privately and render a report up the chain of command. I can recall only 1 event where I was asked to make a sworn deposition defending my—or the stockade's—position on a complaint. It resulted in a clear vindication of our actions and the prisoners making the charge had no basis-in-fact nor competent charge to uphold. Case closed. Naturally, those who rendered the charges acted in consort and were among the 'toughest of the crowd'. . . . LBJ . . . was not run with malice. It was handled with dignity."

The commander of the 18th MP Brigade recalled the difficulties of working with the sort of men sent to him at LBJ.

TOM GUIDERA: "We'd have inspectors come there. I remember one general officer whom I'd known for years. He came and was inspecting the place. He went in one of the [prisoner] tents, and this one good-looking kid [a prisoner] said, 'We can't get any equipment. We can't get any clothing.' The general looked at me. We were on a first-name basis. He said, 'How about that, Tom? What's wrong here?' I said, 'Wait,' and turned to one of . . . the Staff who was accompanying us on the inspection. I said, 'Go get this guy's record.' He brought it and on it was the guy's *signature* for receiving all this equipment. I said, 'Why are you lying to the general?' He said, 'I just felt like it.'

"I'll tell you another anecdote. A lady reporter came to LBJ from the *Overseas Weekly* [newspaper]. We called it the *Oversexed Weekly*. We heard she was going to do an exposé on the place. Tell all the bad things. When she came, I took her in and told her to feel free to talk to inmates. So she talked to inmates, to guards. 'I want to see those conex boxes you use for solitary confinement,' she said. I said, 'Very well.' There was this tent where the boxes had been adapted for solitary confinement. A double row of them with canvas over the top. It was known as Silver City. The guys came out and stood in front of their doors, and she spoke to every one of them. Most of them said, 'Well, I goofed up and ended up in here.' This one guy talked about how he was maltreated. He was pushed around. He pointed to this particular guard who was there, a black NCO, and he said, 'This man abused me.' The guard looked at this woman and said, 'Madame, let me show you where he *bit* me.' He pushed his sleeve up, and the inmate had taken almost a chunk out of the inside of his bicep! What'd we have eventually? Half a million men there? You take half a million men and you'll get a percentage who are no good."

Other commanders, confinement officers, guards, and staff agreed with many of Guidera's attitudes. Occasionally, however, some gave a hint that other employees there quickly developed an "attitude." Clifford Prosser, an NCO at LBJ during 1971, recalled those days.

GUARD PROSSER: "I'm 5′11″ and then weighed about 220 pounds. . . . I was in pretty good shape. . . . We worked twelve-hour shifts and from seven to fifteen days without a day off. In maximum security there wasn't much difference between us and the prisoners. We were all in there. . . . A lot of the guards were not originally MPs but had been reassigned as MPs because of manpower shortages. Even ones who had been trained as MPs didn't necessarily want to be cops. They didn't really have a police mentality, but a military mentality, and a lot of people didn't really want to be there. So it didn't matter whether you were working as a cook or a MP officer or a medic, you may not want to be what you are. So you may not take the responsibility for doing that job well. A lot of the guys working in LBJ didn't have much different of an attitude from a lot of prisoners.

"One thing too, I can inject here. I guess I'm going out on a limb. One thing I've talked to with my wife and friends over the years is that a little bit of what you do and what you become in a situation changes the longer you're in there. And I expect a lot of the guards became pretty adversarial in their outlook the longer they stayed there. If you live in a garbage dump you begin to smell like garbage. You become a little bit more of what you're in. Exposure, and to an extent, the Army wanted you to become that way. I think it was taught, instilled. I've told my wife a number of times. I look back at some of the attitudes I had when I was working there, how defensive, combative I was. I feel the Army used me as an attack dog and I let them do it. I changed my way of thinking to that extent. After I returned home, I was a police officer in Birmingham for fourteen years and I never became that locked in to an attitude. I think it's almost a brainwashing that occurs. I don't know if it's intentional, but I know where I worked over there, there was a lot of that. If it wasn't encouraged, it was at least condoned—to be combative as long as you didn't get anybody in trouble or get your buddy hurt."

# CHAPTER FOUR

# "JUST A BLACK THING"

As the inmate population at LBJ grew almost exponentially, the stockade, built to hold about 400 men, became hopelessly overcrowded. By mid-1968 some 719 men were housed there. The Army accomplished this by the makeshift solution of constantly reducing the square footage allowed for each man. In February 1967 allowable space per man was 70 square feet. By mid-1968 the space was 36.5 square feet. Tents once adequately housed seven men, but by July 1968 each tent contained twice that number. Even getting a bite to eat became a chore for prisoners. Meals were served to 719 inmates in approximately ninety minutes in three to four sittings. Dining room seating capacity was 200, providing a ratio of 3.5 inmates for each seat.

During the entire time that Lieutenant Colonel George Deringer was confinement officer (3 July 1967–4 July 1968), there were no major disturbances at USARVIS. The previous six months, however, had seen a significant increase in possession and use of marijuana and incidents of blacks beating white prisoners. There were thirty-five incidents where inmates were caught using or in possession of marijuana. Thirty-nine men had escaped from the stockade. There had been two cases of sodomy, two of attempted suicide, and six aggravated assaults by blacks against white inmates.

Lieutenant Colonel Deringer remembered some of the problems.

LIEUTENANT COLONEL DERINGER: "One day [at Big Red] a work stoppage occurred. Prisoners milled around testing our determination. I mounted the PT [physical training] stand and talked about the consequences of work refusal. After my talk and Major Jackson's subsequent 'dutch uncle' conversation, the prisoners returned to work filling sandbags. That was the 1st and last potential serious event as best I recall. Needless to say we identified the perpetrators and took suitable segregation procedures.

"We experienced escapes—mainly from work details outside the installation, although on one occassion during the dark of night . . . several cut through the fence after an accomplice from outside threw them a wire cutter. All were apprehended and returned to custody. It was a very personal embarrassment to the whole staff. We tightened our efforts and went on from there.

"[N]o prisoner was ever shot—nor shot at. Only min[imum] custody was allowed out[side the stockade], so shooting an escapee wasn't dictated. . . . Recidivism was VERY COMMON. For those serious offenders—after court-martial—which we simply couldn't handle— a trip back to Leavenworth was necessitated. So a deserving officer and guards would take a trip stateside to deliver. Those excursions went off without a hitch.

"I can tell you this. Those prisoners had 24 hrs daily [to think about] how to beat the system. If we weren't constantly on alert— responding to the least suspicious action—we would have been long gone before our year transpired. It was a year of tension—constant alertness—investigative intrigue—sleepless nights, not knowing when that field phone in the 'hooch' would ring loud and often. . . . Frankly—it was scary over there—within and without. Know what I mean?"

These recollections offered years later contradict Lieutenant Colonel Deringer's response to the situation at the time. As his months in charge of the stockade passed, he saw indications of sufficient unrest to suggest that a major disturbance might break out at any time. Deringer wrote letters requesting that the Army take action to decrease the rapidly growing inmate population and that it increase the number of well-trained guards.

LBJ had not nearly enough staff and guards. According to the "Book," an inmate population of the size ruled over by Deringer required 282 mature, trained, and experienced custodians. Deringer had only 90 personnel actually assigned to him and 63 others in direct support, many of whom did not meet recognized criteria for assignment there. Those 63 were drawn from five other units, thus denying the correctional officer "unity of command," one of the most important principles in the lexicon of war. Furthermore, in grades below E-5, guards were often too youthful and inexperienced, and sometimes were awed by inmates. Prisoners tended to be provocative and belligerent toward them. Such guards either over- or underreacted to the inmates' behavior. The result throughout the LBJ compound was less than adequate control over prisoners.[1]

Aware of these deficiencies, Deringer had approved a proposed modified table of organization and equipment (MTOE), asking that assigned personnel be increased to the "required" 282 men, which had been forwarded to the 89th MP Group. Deringer was also aware of the desperate need for upgrading the physical plant of LBJ. He had asked for and received approval to revamp the compound and, in his last months, two new guard towers were under construction. After his departure, work began in August 1968 on other upgrades. Twenty cells were added to the DSEG building and five fifty-man single floor tropical wooden barracks were erected in the medium security compound, replacing twenty-five tents. Another five fifty-man single floor tropical wooden barracks were built on the west side of LBJ. More showers and latrines were added. The mess hall was upgraded. LBJ would be able to house eight hundred inmates.[2]

Despite these plans, nothing much had actually changed by the time Deringer was reassigned to the States. He had not been able to achieve many of his hopes to improve the physical plant, the mess facilities, or the custodial staff. He still headed a facility that was overcrowded, with prisoners watched by inexperienced guards, and he lacked command authority over all those from other units who bore part of the burden of controlling an increasingly unruly prison population.

---

[1] *DA PAM 20-551* "Staffing Guide for U.S. Army Garrisons."
[2] USARV Inspector General, "Report of Investigation Concerning Alleged Brutality and Maltreatment at the US Army Vietnam Installation Stockade, 1969."

In his last days at LBJ, on 24 June 1968, Deringer submitted a report to the deputy commander, 18th MP Brigade, telling of an assault on whites by blacks on 23–24 June. "Negro" population in B Compound, he said, had an "unruly attitude" and efforts to dampen it had been unsuccessful. He further stated that rumors of Black Power agitation had been heard and that disorders within the compound on 23–24 June lent credence to these rumors. He had, he said, alerted cadre to identify troublemakers. He had increased the guard force in Compound B, redistributed inmates there to break up cliques, and had put seven blacks into DSEG. He had also alerted MP units for possible riot duty. The situation, Deringer said, "was tense, but manageable."

Black Power, to which Deringer referred in his report, had become an issue that rent at the fabric of American society by 1967–1968. Sit-ins at Woolworth lunch counters had long since given way to strident marches on Washington, to riots, to burning of American cities, to the assassinations of black leaders such as Medgar Evers and Martin Luther King. Much of the nation was polarized over these issues and no one had easy answers.

Clenched fist salutes, Afro hairstyles, and such mottos as "Black is beautiful" became symbols of solidarity among African Americans, and they sought to emphasize "black pride" among the people of their race. Talk of upward mobility, of equality before the law, of opportunity—all seemed to blacks nothing more than empty promises that white "slave-masters" used to keep blacks at the very bottom of society. How else to explain the burning and dynamiting of black churches? How else to understand police setting attack dogs loose on peaceful marchers? How else to account for segregation policies that allowed the doors of tax-funded state universities to be slammed in their faces?

Social conflict raging at home soon made its way across the Pacific to American military units assigned to Viet Nam. Black troopers became "brother" to one another, whether they knew each other or not. Their shared color was what mattered. They sported the new Afro hairstyles and grew tiny beards on their lower lips in defiance of military regulations. They developed intricate hand movements to be used when meeting one another, a practice known as "dapping." They believed (sometimes correctly) that they were given the worst fatigue duties and the most dangerous patrol assignments. They objected to the widespread display of Confederate flags in unit offices, particularly when their own "African national flag" was prohibited. Paul Easley, an African American officer and unarguably the finest chaplain I have ever known, was associated with LBJ from 1970 to 1971. He responded to the issue of flags.

CHAPLAIN EASLEY: "I had some problems with guys who had the Confederate flag in their office and then some of the black guys were carrying the little flag they called the Black Flag of Freedom. It's alright for the whites to carry the flag they want, but you blacks can't."

Blacks became incensed at the number of "brothers" who so regularly faced Article 15 company punishment or courts-martial while their white fellows often skated by despite having committed the same or similar offenses. Courts-martial punishments seemed more severe for them than for "whitey" or "chuck," as whites were also known. Blacks seemed ever more suspicious of whites, and they increasingly withdrew into their own subculture, where they could draw strength and encouragement from their "brothers."

Caught unaware, and unprepared for the ferocity of this new and confrontational attitude among Afro-Americans, the Army took too long to respond. The military did not take its first possibly adequate step until 1973, when the Department of Defense established a Race Relations Institute for people of all ranks and all the services at Patrick Air Force Base in Florida. It was almost too little, too late. The war in Viet Nam was over by then.

Lieutenant Colonel Marvin Oberman, confinement officer at LBJ for the first six months of 1967, faced this new and seemingly insoluble racial problem. It grew worse month by month and later haunted George Deringer throughout his yearlong tenure there. The stockade simply teemed with racial hatred.

During the first half of 1968, black inmates outnumbered Caucasians each month except May. That had also been the case for much of 1967, and the trend continued in the years to come. African American inmates focused their attention on their own individual plights, and most came to believe they had been treated unfairly both in their units and at the stockade itself. Most of their guards were white. Although there were always some black guards, a few in positions of real authority at LBJ, the inmates regarded them as "Uncle Toms" and "traitors to their race," deserving of perhaps even more disdain and hatred than their white counterparts.

The only interruption in this climate of increasing racial hatred came during the Tet Offensive that began on 29–30 January 1968, when Viet Cong and North Vietnamese Army units began a country-wide surprise attack on ARVN and American forces. It came to inmates at LBJ in a very personal way when North Vietnamese units attempted to penetrate the huge Long Binh installation. There were tremendous concussions from exploding ammunition dumps set off by satchel charges put in place by enemy infiltrators. Military Police and other units set up perimeter defenses and fought off enemy ground attacks.

Inmates gathered in front of the administration building and surrounded guards. Most were simply frightened and wondered what to do if the compound was overrun. Others begged to be given weapons to protect themselves or to be allowed out to join in the general fighting. Lieutenant Colonel Deringer noted that "[E]mergency plans were in order to evacuate if necessary." No serious thought was given to inmate requests for arms, and the danger posed by the attack gradually faded. Yet for a time, black and white prisoners had put aside their animosities in the face of this action by their common enemy.

The peace did not last. Tension returned as the days passed. Within the compound, almost palpable racial tensions again built between blacks and whites. Although they may have been more unbridled at USARVIS, similar animosities existed systemwide. In December 1972, the Department of Defense issued a four-volume report. On the matter of race it stated: "No command or installation is entirely free from the effects of systematic discrimination against minority servicemen."[3]

The Congressional Black Caucus noted that African Americans represented 12.1 percent of all enlisted personnel but 16.3 percent

---

[3]Department of Defense, *Report of the Task Force on the Administration of Military Justice* (4 vols., Washington, D.C.: Government Printing Office, 1972), Vol. 1, pp. 19–20.

of those in combat. Of those who ran afoul of the *UCMJ*, despite constituting but 12 percent of the population, blacks were dispropor-tionately represented, receiving 25 percent of all Article 15 punish-ments. Blacks received 23.4 percent of punitive discharges as a result of general and special courts-martial as opposed to 16.9 percent of whites. One of every seven black soldiers in 1971 received less-than-honorable discharges. Whites received one out of fourteen. And in Viet Nam 31 percent of blacks received combat assignments as opposed to 18 percent of whites. Clearly, something was wrong with the system.[4]

Racial hatred within the Army was perhaps as clearly evident at LBJ as anywhere. One inmate, an African American, recalled those days in maximum security.

INMATE PRIVATE NATHANIEL FORT JR.: "Blacks were going through an identity thing . . . . Every day everybody would shout out their name, the state they came from. That's the way they communi-cated. I saw a lot of wrong things [done] to whites in there. Blacks were very militant in there about things. . . . [W]hen blacks was havin' what they call roll-call every day, durin' that roll call, whites had to ask permission to flush the toilet. Or they got hurt. It was bad. What they did. They had connections. They knew how to open the cells. Them guys were some slick guys. They could open those cells and come right in your cell and get you. . . . If they didn't get you then, they'd get you when they let us out to play basketball for maybe half an hour to get some sunlight, for we was in maximum security and there wasn't no light in there."

Another African American spoke of even lower levels of tolerance.

INMATE PRIVATE GREGG PAYTON: "[W]hite boys really had to take a low profile in the stockade. They were greatly outnum-bered; there was a lot of hatred, nobody was toleratin' any white boys bein' in control.

"Most of us were young men, we were duped into goin' to Viet

---

[4]Congressional Black Caucus, *Racism in the Military: A New System for Rewards and Punishment* (Washington, D.C.: Government Printing Office, 1972). See also William R. Rae, Stephen B. Forman, and Howard C. Olsen, *Future Impact of Dissident Elements Within the Army on the Enforcement of Discipline, Law and Order* (Technical Paper #RAC-TP-441. McLean, Va.: Research Analysis Corporation, 1972), p. 41.

Nam. We really didn't have the whole script in on why we were there. When we went over there we really began to find out we were pawns. We really began to get a little bit about our history and what this thing was all about. A lot of anger as related to white people. A whole race of people whose consciousness was being raised. For so long black African Americans didn't have any idea of what their history was all about. As we began to recognize we were being pawns, we didn't want nothing to do with it. There was an angriness.

"Black and white guys may have fought well together out in the boonies but it's only out of necessity . . . . Black guys hung out with black guys because of identification. . . . [T]he military made me a racist. I wasn't born [one] but I recognize now that I'm an African American who lives in a racist society.

"A 'chuck' was a white boy. . . . That's what we used to call them. Yeah, chucks."

A white social worker at the prison observed the racial discontent.

WAYNE PRICE: "There were some race riots . . . . One was a little one in '67 prior to my arrival. I think a couple of people got killed. . . . [I]t was overcrowded; 70 percent black at least. Significantly higher number of blacks. Draw your own conclusions from that. Make one wonder if something wasn't quite right. Maybe military justice was a little racist-oriented."

A chaplain saw what was happening.

CHAPLAIN VERNON SWIM: "There was a lot of racial tension. You could feel it going one direction or the other depending on whether there were more black or whites. A lot of dapping going on. If the blacks held power, they'd stand in the gateway and block it up while they were dapping. That would infuriate the whites, who not only had to stand there and watch it, but couldn't get through the gate until they got through dapping."

Dapping constantly irritated the whites—prisoners, guards, and staff. A white supply clerk put it this way.

MP KEN COWAN: "It was a problem when you'd go to eat. You'd get up to the food line and here were all these blacks slappin' and dappin'. It'd last for about five minutes. So I'd just walk around and cut in front of them and they'd get all ticked off but I didn't put up with it. 'Hey, you guys can play with each other all you want, but I came here to eat.'

"I went over to the day room one time [at the 284th MP Company] and inside were all these black people, MPs. So I stood around and watched, and what it was was a Black Panther meeting. That's a fact. There was a lot of racial tension. They were handing out pamphlets on how to start a revolution."

A confinement officer had doubts about Cowan's recollection of black MPs holding such a meeting.

LIEUTENANT COLONEL WILLAM KEYES: "I think the story of holding a Black Panther meeting in the [MP] day room is a war story. I wouldn't believe it."

Fed up with the black dapping, some whites decided to strike back. A white MP told what happened.

SERGEANT JOHNNY COURTHERS: "The races were polarized. The blacks had their 'dap' routine, so white prisoners made up their version of it, too, integrating the peace sign into it."

Animosity was not just verbal. A white inmate recalled how he was treated by blacks.

PRIVATE TERRY SMOOT: "Our biggest threat . . . wasn't the guards but the blacks. They made homemade knives and traveled in gangs. . . . I'm a little man, about 5´3˝ or 5´4˝. In my cowboy boots I might be 5´5˝. One black chose me to pick on and I'd pass him by and he'd take something and rap me over the head with it. I was planning how to get him, but in the meantime I had to take his abuse."

A black inmate who was imprisoned in the summer of 1968 had this to say.

PRIVATE JEREMIAH JAMES: "LBJ had guys from all the divisions in Vietnam, but most of them were from the 101st Airborne. They was combat hardened. Their nerves were real bad. . . . Lots of stuff was going on back in the States—campus unrest, the racial situation, the death of Martin Luther King. And so lots of stuff was going on inside LBJ too. Four guys were beaten to death by other inmates. It was purely racial motivation.

"One young white guy I know. He had baby features, didn't shave. You ever know anyone you liked from the first beginning? He was like that. He was nice to me. He talked to me. They killed him that night. They covered his head with a blanket and beat him with sticks from the cots. He never said a word. They beat him to death simply because he was white. This still bothers me today. I still hurt from that.

"Another white guy showed pictures of his wife or girlfriend who was black. He got beat to death. You could cut the tension inside the wire . . . with a knife."

Racial hatred at LBJ was not just a phenomenon of the late 1960s. It continued until the prison was finally closed in 1973. One young man—an SP-4—who worked at LBJ as a social worker (MOS 91-Golf) became a chaplain years later. When interviewed, he remembered the hatred he had observed during his months at LBJ from October 1971 to June 1972.

SOCIAL WORKER KERRY STEEDLEY: "There was a lot of racism among the inmates, and where you [mainly] saw that was in maximum security. . . . [Those inmates] seethed in their anger til they got to Leavenworth. . . . A lot of it had racial overtones. . . . One morning I went through maximum security, and two black guards had just finished taking care of a black prisoner in such a way that even if he had reported [the incident], they left no marks on him. . . . I remember one incident. The night before [some blacks] had started a Black Power chant. It would go from cell to cell, passing it to the next guy. This white guy refused to do it because there were some racial things in it. The next morning during their PT a couple of black guys worked him over while they were supposed to be filing out. Two black guards found out about it. They took the black . . . ringleader and did a job on him and got his attention."

A guard who served at LBJ in 1971 while Steedley was there also remembered those "roll calls."

SERGEANT CLIFF PROSSER: "I heard a lot of black roll call shouting. They did it anytime they wanted to show their unity. They all talked about how the revolution was coming. That was the big thing. The favorite thing they called us was 'swine.' Back in the States police officers were 'pigs,' over there we were 'swine.' Or they'd call white prisoners 'dogs' and say, 'When I get back in the World, I'm

gonna find out where you live. Kill your family.' The first couple
of times you hear that, it kind of blows you away. You don't ever
entirely take it as being harmless. . . . Course they had the dapping
thing they did with their hands. A lot of verbal tensions, racial tensions. I didn't see a lot of organization to it in the cell blocks. No real
serious attempts on guards' lives. . . . They talked about [revenge] a
lot, but they do in every jail. A lot of it was just smoke."

Inmate James B. Vaughan's time at LBJ overlapped that of both
Steedley and Prosser. He was held there in pretrial confinement for
forty-two days from late 1971 to early 1972. He told a story that
related to those evening Black Power chants.

INMATE VAUGHAN: "We were in the new LBJ. . . . There were
like four block houses in the max[imum security area] and they were
mainly black. . . . I'd say it was two-thirds black. . . . There were a lot
of NCOs in there busted down to E-1 for assaulting officers out in
the field. There were a lot of guys in there for murder, for killing
their lieutenants—anything to do with max was assault—you killed
somebody or tried to kill somebody or beat up on somebody. The
only other people they kept in there were ones in protective custody;
like somebody was going to testify against somebody else. . . . The
blacks called it the 'black house' instead of the 'block house.'"

Vaughan recalled that blacks called the medium security compound, in which a number of whites were held, the "dog pound."

INMATE VAUGHAN: "You were a dog if you were white. . . . [I]n
the max security, when the lights go out every night, all the blacks
started calling: '*Roll call in the black house. Roll call in the black house.*'
They'd do that for about twenty minutes. Then they'd start:'*Black
house A, cell number one.*' They all gave themselves Moslem names.
'*Brother Abdul, hometown and state. More better black power in this
here black house.*' They'd do this every night—sixty guys doing it—
and they couldn't remember their [Muslim] names from one night
to the next. Then they'd go on a verbal barrage of the whites: '*Hang
youselves, dogs.*' One time they rattled a white guy, and the sucker
hung himself. I was a trustee and they'd go: '*You white motherfucker.
I'm going to kill your motherfucking white ass.*' So I'd shout back,
'*Come on superman. Just bust through them bars.*'

"I'm 6′2″ and probably weighed 120–130 pounds. . . . When I was a trustee I was segregated from other prisoners in max. The guards thought maybe I couldn't protect myself I was so skinny."

As a trustee, one of Vaughan's responsibilities was to feed other inmates in maximum security.

"God, man, for a month I had to get up and get dressed at 4 or 4:30—an hour earlier than everyone else. We were locked up individually. There were two [of us] from every cell block and they had around twenty-three cells in each one. Then we had to go over [to the mess hall] and put meals on trays. We had these big metal carts on which we could load twenty or thirty food trays. We had these Army fiber–looking cups and pitchers of coffee. I don't remember if we had little cartons of milk. We had to go around and serve all the prisoners . . . and then go back and pick up all the stuff and take it back."

After being shouted at and threatened by black inmates one evening, Vaughan had a speech prepared for them the next day as he served them their food.

"'This has some of my urine or spittle in it.' They didn't give me a whole lot of trouble."

Guards had their own set of problems with this racism. One MP officer expressed their difficulties.

JAMES PEDERSON: "Remember, [guards] were all young men, some not so mature. . . . After a time they began to knuckle under pressure from prisoners or they became tense and involved in verbal conflicts. Particularly if one was a black guard . . . prisoners asked why they served. They were under constant pressure. . . . Harassed as traitors to their own race, doing things for white people. . . . A couple of black guards who were extraordinarily good, after a time came to me and said, 'Sir, I'd like to be moved somewhere else because it's starting to get to me.'"

A former chaplain, a black man who preferred not to be identified, objected to then-prevailing white attitudes toward those of his race that he saw regularly when he served in Viet Nam.

"Conditions were bad. Any condition—if you're in prison—is not good. No matter what kind of improvements might have been made in the conditions, for the person who came in next week who was not there last week, it is all terrible. I think just the fact you're in jail in a combat situation is bad."

This chaplain commented that "one of the protests [at LBJ] was led by a white guy who was bitching about conditions of the jail. . . . [I]f you want to survive in the midst of all that kind of distress, you get out there and lead some protests or you'll be identified as a guest of the establishment."

This former chaplain also saw occasional hopeful signs.

"[At one point t]hey had a riot, and they used to have these more often than I'm comfortable with even thinking about. These black guys were jumping on this white guy. A black inmate came to his rescue. Why? His answer was, 'Man, this guy's a jumper [an airborne-qualified soldier] . . . and them damn legs [infantrymen] was fighting him.' . . . I was moved by that. Brotherhood in the midst of . . . violence."

Chaplain Paul Easley thought some of the racial problem may have been due simply to the different language used by blacks and whites.

"The key was the cultural lingo. . . . Some guy from Chicago would say, 'I'm gonna kill yo' ass.' That meant 'I'm pissed off at you.' White unit commanders didn't understand and therefore would recommend courts-martial."

While there was undoubted truth in Easley's remark, it fails to convey the depths of antagonism that separated the races. Both white and black inmates remember there was a great deal more racism evident at LBJ than the chaplain admitted to. Although black-white antagonism seeped through much of the prison population in general, certain prisoners of both races bore particularly careful watching. These were the incorrigibles.

Such men were regularly remanded to the maximum detention area of LBJ, and their guards were always wary of them. Many of these were stone killers, egocentric, needing immediate gratification for sudden desires, devoid of any ability to feel the pain of others or, indeed, even to feel that others were real. They would have been in trouble with the law had they never gone to Viet Nam and some, years after their return, are still locked away from society for their crimes or disturbed behavior. The provost marshal for the 18th MP Brigade, who later became warden of the Iowa State Penitentiary, told of one such man.

CRISPUS NIX: "The prisoner . . . was a Marine . . . named Fountain. . . . He was just a crazy sonofabitch. A Marine named Mahoney apprehended Fountain—I think it was in Okinawa. . . . Fountain had locked himself in his cell and I wanted to use foam on him rather than tear gas, so my boss said, 'What if he dies?' And I said, 'Well, I don't give a damn.' He wouldn't let me do it. We finally got two fire-hoses after everybody went to sleep, coupling them together. We were able to force Fountain up against the wall and . . . overpower him. . . . When he got to the DB [Disciplinary Barracks] he took a hostage— an Air Force guy—and had a knife around the guy's throat, carried him up to the gate. . . . And then we finally sent him to the Feds. . . . When he was in the Feds he killed several people. He was at Marion for awhile and now he's down at Springfield in Missouri. He has a special cell with its own self-contained exercise area. I've kept up with him because he loves me so."

An SP-4 supply clerk who served at LBJ in 1971 told of another.

KEN COWAN: "I saw a lot of sick things happen inside the prison wire. One of the sickest things I ever heard was this guy who told me how he tried to kill his company commander. [laughs] This is cold. 'I was sick of the guy,' he said. 'I hated him. So I set up a bunch of clay-mores around his underground hooch, and when he walked out I blew him up—blew his legs and arms off. He's still alive but he's a vegetable. Everything was going okay, until I messed up. [While he was recuperating] I sent him a get-well card and a free dance course to Arthur Murray's dance studio, and they caught up with me.'"

An MP Private First Class told of one cold-blooded killer who seemed to have utterly no remorse.

GUARD THOMAS MCKEON: "One of the guys in a conex told a buddy of his that he was there on a bum rap. His M-79 had gone off accidentally three or four times, killing his whole squad. The M-79 is a single shot weapon."

A Judge Advocate General officer long remembered one prisoner he had known at LBJ.

CAPTAIN BEN YUDESIS: "One inmate . . . Billy Smith from the First CAV Division, fragged officers and was charged with murder. Very quiet. The coldest set of eyes I ever remember. Tall guy. Well over six foot. Abnormally long arms. He stayed in close hold most of the time. Never turn your back on that cell when going down that corridor."

Such men, in their own way, could be fascinating. Psychologists have long tried to understand how their minds work. Social Work Specialist Wayne Price was interested in the pathology of prisoners and often talked at length with them.

WAYNE PRICE: "One of the questions I asked was 'How is it you got here?' One interesting story was where two guys got angry and got in a fight throwing grenades around their company area at each other. . . . I remember we had one of the more decorated guys in Viet Nam there. Lot of medals for combat stuff. He just decided not to do it anymore. He quit. They took offense to that. A [guy] in maximum security was accused of killing a Vietnamese woman. I don't remember the details. . . . Most of them were military-oriented crimes—sleeping on guard duty, AWOL—more than drugs. In '67 there weren't that many drugs around. A little marijuana and alcohol, some opium, amphetamines. Heroin came in later, '69 or '70.'"

It was always easy for those behind the wire to find excuses to explain why they were there. Only a few were able to really believe that it was their own fault. Others were always ready to blame something else: the system, unfeeling officers, too-rigid noncoms. One inmate put it this way.

TERRY EDWARD SMOOT: "I was an inmate between April and June 1971. . . . I was sent there for assault on my captain, first sergeant, chief of firing battery, chief of gun section, assistant chief of gun section, and two PFCs. I was in a fit of rage, like a blackout. . . . Military lawyers, military judges, military prosecutors, military witnesses. Everything was military. It had to be biased. . . . . I had been up for quite awhile, and the captain sent word that he wanted to see me. I sent back word that I was going to sleep for a couple of hours and then I'd be up to see him. I went to bed. The first sergeant came in and grabbed me out of my bunk and things just went black. When I waked up I was tied to a post. I tried to untie myself and he came along and jerked the rope tight. I spit in his face and told him I was going to kill the motherfucker before I left Nam. Then the MPs came. One specification was hitting the first sergeant with my fist and kicking him in the groin. Disobeying an order. Striking my chief of gun section and kicking him in the chest. Drunk and disorderly in quarters. Wrongfully and willfully discharging a firearm under circumstances that would endanger life. Wrongfully communicating a threat to kill. . . . Several of these charges were reduced or dropped. . . . They got me for assault, but in my eyes it was self-defense. . . . Do I think the punishment was appropriate? No, I don't. I shouldn't have been court-martialed at all. I was having a medical—not a criminal—breakdown, and I was treated criminally."

The stockade at Long Binh contained many men like these as July 1968 began. As the days ticked away, both Lieutenant Colonel George Deringer and his executive officer, Major Norwood Jackson, prepared to depart Long Binh for new assignments elsewhere. Deringer believed that he had done a good job.

GEORGE DERINGER: "There are no skeletons. Oh hell, I suppose events escape my memory after 22-23 years, but I'm a very proud former corrections officer who in retrospect wouldn't change a thing basically from the operation in '67–'68. I received accolades from nearly every CO or his rep who visited the stockade. *It was* well run and the mission accomplished. We were *FIRM*. We were *FAIR*. But, get out of line and you suffer the consequences—within the limits of 'the book.'"

Deringer's replacement as confinement officer was Lieutenant Colonel Vernon D. Johnson. He took over on 5 July 1968. In just fifty-five days his world would come crashing down.

# CHAPTER FIVE

# "DRUGS WERE A REAL PROBLEM"

The arrival of Lieutenant Colonel Vernon D. Johnson as the new confinement officer was a turning point in the life of LBJ. He came with good credentials. A later temporary confinement officer told about him.

MP LIEUTENANT COLONEL EUGENE MURDOCK: "Johnson was the only real penologist of the whole damn bunch. He's got his doctorate in penology. He's a judo expert; a black belter."

Not everyone, however, was pleased with the Military Police Corps' choice in selecting Lieutenant Colonel Johnson for his position at the stockade. Major Norwood Jackson, Deringer's executive officer, had been intimately involved for a year in the actual day-to-day operations of USARVIS. He felt that in many ways he was the one actually in charge and sometimes acted accordingly. He had heard of Johnson through the Military Police Corps' gravevine and had serious doubts about the man's ability to head a tension-filled prison facility.

MAJOR NORWOOD JACKSON: "It was very devastating. . . . They put Vern Johnson in after I warned that he was not the guy to put in there. He was a very learned person but no common sense. . . . [H]e began to allow inmates to go around the staff. He began to think he could handle anything and didn't allow people to use the authority they had. . . . He was the kind of guy who, in the face of the staff, would take an inmate's word for something. That's hard on discipline. . . . [H]e liked to impress [others] with his knowledge but he had a problem dealing with people face-to-face. . . . He felt he knew it all. . . . [T]hey lost all control because the inmates bypassed them. Johnson . . . would chastise, countermand orders, and take the word of inmates over staff. He chastised staff in front of inmates. Exactly what I heard happened."

Jackson's sentiments were echoed by another confinement officer who served from November 1968 to November 1969 and who knew Johnson.

LIEUTENANT COLONEL WILLIAM KEYES: "As far as I'm concerned [Vern Johnson] was Father Murphy or Father Flanagan. 'There's no such thing as a bad boy.' The hell there isn't. I've seen some real wizards in my day. . . ."

A clerk in the LBJ administration section who served under Lieutenant Colonel Johnson recalled what LBJ was like when the new confinement officer arrived in early July 1968:

MP MIKE DOHERTY: "[He] was of a liberal persuasion and believed in rehabilitation. He had recreational programs for the inmates like baseball, softball, weight lifting. He believed he had good rapport with inmates but during my first two months there, the prisoners *ran* the stockade. They made their own moonshine hooch, faked injuries, refused to work; they'd go to the infirmary to get exempted from work. They hated going to work at Big Red. They pretty much did what they wanted.

"They complained about the lousy food, but we ate the same things. They complained because of overcrowding. There was always tension. . . . There was very little discipline."

It was not that Johnson did not have good support staff. He did. He had counselors to listen to prisoners and to work with them to try to resolve their complaints. Although he served at a later time, after Johnson was gone, one social worker has given a good description of what he and all his fellows tried to do.

WAYNE PRICE: "[A] social work specialist provided some counseling, did the initial and subsequent work-ups prior to professional staff seeing them. Evaluation work, intake histories if a person needed to see professional staff. Providing support and doing general assistant social work at times, either counseling or doing preliminary work before seeing a psychologist or psychiatrist.... I'd try to get an impression from inmates whether their thinking was clear and their associations relevant. I had such a short period of time to do that after the orientations.

"I told them we were there and that we provided counseling and if anyone had problems they could check with me. I would tell them how to get in touch with the professionals.... [A]s everyone was walking out the door, I'd touch base with them, ask them three or four questions. [If I thought they had] emotional or psychiatric problems I'd ask their names and tell them I'd be getting in touch with them. Then I'd have them come over to my office."

Another social worker, a Specialist Fourth Class who served at LBJ from October 1971 to June 1972, added his recollections to those of Price.

KERRY STEEDLEY: "I had just graduated from our denominational school, Free Will Baptist Bible College, Nashville, Tennessee.... I'd left a wife and baby boy and I was homesick.... I had grown up in a southern, Christian . . . sheltered environment. [Viet Nam gave me a] sense of being overwhelmed and intimidated.... It was awakening to a side of life I had never seen.... [T]he enemy I saw over there were drugs, rebellion against authority, draftees who didn't want to be there, the racial issues.... I was assigned to an MP company.... I had never done any drugs. All I knew about them came from a little reading I had done in school.

"One of the things I resented was that counselors had to pull guard duty.... The guys I worked with saw me in one role—a buffer between the guards and the command . . . trying to be sympathetic, listen to their story, try to help them with what personal career or legal things they need—and then they look up during lunchtime and see their counselor in a tower with a shotgun. I didn't like that."

Such mixed roles seem to have been the rule rather than the exception at LBJ. A Judge Advocate General captain who served at Long Binh while Steedley was there commented on the same problem.

BEN YUDESIS: "We had disturbances in the stockade but none that lasted more than a couple of hours. One happened in the medium compound .... about 0330-0400.... The early morning shift cooks were refusing to fall out.... I pulled the guards out so there wouldn't be a hostage situation. We'd already called the reaction force ... and [it] was coming through the front gate. [E]nlisted people from the counseling section—with their helmets and clubs—were making up about half the front rank .... It wasn't really what counselors were supposed to be doing. We pulled them out, and the rest of the reaction force went in and quieted things down real quick."

SOCIAL WORK SPECIALIST KERRY STEEDLEY: "Some [inmates] should not have been there, but most were deservedly sent to LBJ.... LBJ's reputation was a tough place. People knew when they got there they'd have to toe the line or there'd be some consequences.... We were looked at as the softies because sometimes we would take the case of an inmate and be an advocate and sometimes the staff resented that."

One chaplain, who served at the Marine Stockade in Da Nang rather than at LBJ, summed up attitudes prevalent at both facilities.

RALPH LUDWIG: "The MPs saw the inmates as criminals. Social workers saw them as people who came from bad families. Educational specialists saw them as people who didn't have an education and therefore needed educational opportunities. Psychologists saw them as people who had personality disorders that they needed to work through. Lawyers saw them as people worked over by the [military] criminal justice system. The commander saw these guys as degenerates and an embarrassment to the Army. All these different people saw these folk from a different light.

"Social workers didn't talk to education people, education people didn't talk to the lawyers, lawyers didn't talk to anybody except their clients, and MPs wanted to incarcerate and punish them. There was no communication between the specialties."

Chaplains earnestly tried to help the inmates with whom they came in contact.

CHAPLAIN VERNON SWIM: "I was ... shocked when I found out what my assignment was going to be for I had never worked with an MP group before. I knew Infantry and Armor, but not MP.... The guy who told me of the assignment said, 'Vern, we're going to keep you real safe in Viet Nam. In fact, we're going to keep you so safe we're going to lock you up'. . . . I got a bunch of band instruments from Special Services because I discovered there was a lot of talent. [Inmates] came over [to the chapel] in the evening when they were free and got the instruments out. They got quite a band going. I would [also] use them in [my religious] services.

"I had some excellent conversion experiences with those guys. I know prisoners are real manipulators; can't always tell what's legitimate, but I felt there was some real legitimate changing of directions in fellows' lives while I was there. I had no real follow-up on them after they left.

"Guys in maximum were allowed out of their cells for chapel. They were escorted by guards. The chapel was just across the wire from maximum confinement. But when [racial] tensions were too high, they assembled them in the maximum confinement compound and we'd have services there."

INMATE PRIVATE JAMES VAUGHAN: "I made use of the chapel. When I was in max, the choir members in the chapel came from max. That was the only time when you were a prisoner that you could get out of max, was Sunday to go to church. That was the only time, and I sang in that choir every Sunday. I talked to the chaplain. You'd have a little choir practice so you'd get out of a little . . . bullshit they'd want you to do."

SOCIAL WORK SPECIALIST KERRY STEEDLEY: "I used to go to chapel and listen to Chaplain Vern Swim, a Nazarene. He had a service inside the stockade. There were another two or three chaplains [for the rest of] Long Binh. I went to both services, one inside, one outside. At the time I wasn't sure what God wanted me to do. The things that happened made me think seriously of becoming a chaplain. It was through observing their ministry that caused me to get out of the Army with the intention of going to seminary. . . . I think there were at least a few people I helped."

CHAPLAIN WAYNE KING: "When I was DEROSing [returning] from Viet Nam we landed at Travis Air Force Base about two in the morning. I took a taxi to San Francisco International Airport and there was *nobody* there at three in the morning. I was walking across this darkened terminal, and suddenly I hear this guy shout 'Chaplain King!' I saw this guy in an Ivy League suit. 'Do I know you?' 'Yeah. I was an inmate at LBJ.' I'd talked to him about faith. He said, 'Some of the things you said to me got through to me. It didn't look like it, and you didn't think you were getting through to me but you were. I finished my six months at the retraining brigade at Fort Riley.' He went straight, got out, and went to work for IBM. How? He said, 'They decided to take a chance on me. I credit you with getting through to me.'"

The major problem facing Lieutenant Colonel Johnson and his administration was the free flow of drugs coming inside the wire at LBJ. This had been a problem from the first days of Pershing Field, on through all the years at Long Binh, and then again during the final days back at Pershing. Try as they might, commanders, staff, and guards could not prevent inmates from dosing themselves with whatever came readily to hand.

Much was obtained surreptitiously; some was sold openly. John Berry in his book, *Those Gallant Men*, writes: "I have very vague recollections of . . . the sale of 'repacks'—American cigarette packages in which the final inch of each cigarette had been replaced with marijuana, and the altered cigarettes had been repacked—nineteen to a package—and sold on post" (p. 85).

One director of custody described the inmates' frantic efforts to obtain a "high."

JAMES PEDERSON: "Prisoners would do anything to try to get drugs. They'd do *wild* things. They would take plastic forks and hold them against a cigarette til they smoked, breathe that, and try to get high. Prisoners would wipe feces on their cigarettes and smoke them to try to get high. They couldn't control themselves [and] were so wild at times that they were very difficult [for us] to control."

CHAPLAIN VERNON SWIM: "We had a group of prisoners in to paint the inside of the new chapel shortly after I got there. One of the guys disappeared, and we couldn't locate him. Then I found him in the bathroom, zonked out. He had gone in there and taken some gasoline and poured it in the toilet and stuck his head in there to get high on the gas and passed out with his head in the toilet."

INMATE PRIVATE TERRY SMOOT: "We tried various ways of getting high. We heard dried banana peels would to it and tried them, but they weren't too effective. Or we'd take ten deep breaths and then have someone squeeze us and we'd go out for a few seconds. That was the most common thing to do. I did manage to talk one of the MPs into giving me a matchbox full of marijuana and I got five joints out of it."

INMATE PRIVATE NATHANIEL FORT JR.: "The guys would do anything to get high. I'm serious, man, they would smoke the wrap around a cigarette paper; they'd roll that up and smoke it. They'd soak a cigarette in that stripe toothpaste—Pepsodent?—and smoke that. I guess they was just crazy."

MP MAJOR NORWOOD JACKSON: "There were a lot of substance abusers there. When people are scared they use substances more readily. Drugs came in there. We had no way of stopping it. . . . We patrolled the area pretty heavily. We put in a double-apron fence with twelve or fourteen feet of space between them, a seven-foot fence with razor ribbon, so nobody was going to penetrate that. If you get hung up on it, it'll make a soprano of you. There might have been instances when somebody rode by on a jeep and threw a packet over the fence, but we had towers and we could pretty much see and control. Inmates were housed in such a way that nobody had direct access to them."

CHAPLAIN VERNON SWIM: "I know we had a helicopter one time flew over and threw out a bunch of drugs. Supply by air. People could pass things through the wire. Ninety percent of those inside were there on drug-related charges. Or drugs were related somewhere in their charges."

CHAPLAIN RALPH LUDWIG: "Drugs were a problem . . . . One guy had been in solitary confinement for weeks but got drugs the whole time he was there. Guys were strip-searched, but still they came in. Some guards were accused of bringing drugs in to the prisoners. The Army was not aware of the extent of drug usage or sophisticated enough to know the lengths to which people would go to get them."

INMATE PRIVATE GREGG PAYTON: "Some guards provided us with all kinds of good marijuana. A lot of guards didn't search us that good when we'd come back from work details. Or guys would come to visit friends in the stockade and bring drugs. So it wasn't that big of a deal. I had a lot of things going for me—plenty of drugs, a support system around me, so it was no problem for me.

"One of the guys I trained with [at Fort Dix] was . . . one of the tower guards. . . . So when we'd go out on police call every morning, I would position myself so I could walk right under his tower and in the course of the night he had dropped pills or a joint down and he'd say 'to the right,' and guide me to it."

INMATE PRIVATE RUDOLPH GRAY: "There was some drugs [as early as 1967]. The guards might bring in reefers. They was plentiful. Pills—yes. Opium—no. Who knows? Not to my knowledge about the opium. Somebody at night would come by and throw marijuana over the fence."

MP SERGEANT MARION POWERS, NCO IN CHARGE OF MAXIMUM SECURITY: "I was a naive twenty-one-year-old and didn't know what marijuana was. I had taken a work detail out . . . to fill sandbags. They'd carry leftover empty bags back to the compound so the Vietnamese wouldn't steal them overnight. This one young guy, eighteen or nineteen, wanted to carry the empty sacks. They'd stuff the empties into one and carry one back. He'd worked out something with Vietnamese in the area who were working close to where we were. They'd holler back and forth and me, not understanding, I didn't know what they were saying. Thought they were just having a good time. [But] he had this deal where they placed a sandbag of marijuana where he could pick it up and carry it back. So he carries a full sack of marijuana back into the stockade. I didn't know. I found out later because I got my ass chewed out."

INMATE VAUGHAN: "[T]he doctor was this . . . worm dick. I don't remember his name. He was short, fat, curly hair, and wore glasses. Such a chicken shit. He was so intimidated by the black prisoners that when they'd say, 'Doc, give me some Dalmane or Reds or something,' he'd write it out. And the guards would have to come by and dispense it to them. When the guys would go to court-martial, they had MPs that would let them get high and they'd come back so full of heroin they'd be nodded out all over the place."

CAPTAIN YUDESIS: "[For a time] it was pretty easy for prisoners to get narcotics in the confinement facility. Parolees or guards brought them in. They did everything. Heroin came in little capsules about the size of the first joint on your little finger. Guys would know they were going inside and they'd put those capsules up their rectum—but they usually popped out on the strip search in the sally port."

GUARD SERGEANT SAM MULLIN: "Inmates lie if they say MPs were their suppliers. They were liars! I would have heard of it. . . . Most MPs looked at prisoners as assholes . . . and wouldn't have helped them. They either got them on work details or when mama-sans threw drugs over the fence to them. . . . They were low-lifes. We took the worst the units had."

Unfortunately, it was not only inmates who abused drugs. The drug problem became widespread as American involvement in Viet Nam increased, and even spread to some degree into MP units. One guard, a member of the 284th MP Company at Long Binh, put it this way.

MP KEN COWAN: "There was a drug problem in our unit. You could buy a vial of heroin the size of a thimble for $2 that was 96–98 percent pure. . . . Some bases I heard of were literally three-quarter addicted. . . . You could get a big baggie of weed for $5. People . . . did [it] in their hooches, and no one ever busted anybody. . . . [P]eople would sometimes get too wasted and forget where they were and leave a vial of heroin on their beds. I'd go over to another person's hooch after hours and there'd be two or three people there smoking dope. Higher than a kite. . . . I stayed away from drugs out of my religious background. I'm LDS, Mormon."

Cowan's view was reinforced by another MP who served at LBJ.

SERGEANT CLIFFORD PROSSER: "Heroin was absolutely rampant over there. [That's] something you don't hear too much about anymore. . . . A tremendous amount used. In any latrine over there—in MP companies as well as infantry units—[you could] look through the hole and see hundreds of little plastic thumb-size jugs, somewhat larger than a thimble, that had held heroin. It was a problem for everybody. Use of it became a [real] problem. . . . When you get a guy over there spending $20–25 a day for low-cost, good-quality heroin, and he has to come back to the United States . . . come up with $250–300 a day for the same stuff, there's got to be a serious problem. . . . One of my best friends . . . was a heroin addict. That was about the worst thing in Vietnam. He was only nineteen."

Another officer sadly recalled how bad the drug situation was.

CAPTAIN YUDESIS: "We had one guy six months, dried out completely. His sentence had expired. People from his unit came and picked him up to take him to the 90th Replacement and ship him home. They were driving him over to Finance, about a mile away, to pick up his back pay and outprocess, and he OD'd in Finance and died. Where the hell he got hold of the stuff nobody seemed to know—or would admit."

GUARD PROSSER: "You hear a lot about the use of marijuana and [see it] played up in the movies. But there was a lot of hard drugs . . . and at least two of [every] five prisoners I had in my block were either in on drug charges or were having to withdraw from drugs when in on a different charge. Basically it was a cold turkey kind of thing. That was one of the changes I saw. The military began treating withdrawals with Thorazine and other drugs that reduced cramps and other effects of withdrawal. We put them in a cell for a long time with no belts and nothing they could hurt themselves with. Suicide attempts were anticipated. I did see the military start to lean more toward medical treatment. No use of methadone that I know of, but they talked about it. . . . I don't have any first-hand knowledge where inmates got drugs.

"One of the most common pain medications . . . was Darvon compound. A large capsule with a kernel of pure Darvon diluted with aspirin powder. Prisoners learned to take that thing apart and take the Darvon out. They could get a pretty good hit."

One man who was an inmate during the summer of 1971 told of his own experiences in Viet Nam's rampant drug culture.

INMATE PRIVATE ROBERT JACKSON: "I just plain got too far on drugs to help myself and it got me into this mess. I was arrested with *a lot* of heroin, two hundred vials . . . . Drugs [at LBJ] were available but not a problem. Scarce. The only [ones] I knew of came in by guards. . . . When I first went to LBJ they offered me medical help to withdraw from heroin. I accepted and ended up going straight to solitary for five days to cold turkey from a *real* heavy heroin addiction. The medic who came by when I was withdrawing from heroin laughed right along with the guard who was with him.... They jeered and asked me if I wanted another shot of heroin."

Another inmate from Florida remembered his own problems.

INMATE NATHANIEL FORT JR.: "I was stationed at Ford Ord for a year before I went to Vietnam. That's where I got turned on to a lot of different drugs. This little town, Sanford, where I grew up—there wasn't no drugs—well, now there is, but when I was growin' up the strongest thing you could get was a Coca-Cola and a BC [headache powder]. We thought we was doin' somethin'. We was just beer drinkers. We was just boys. Didn't know nothin' about drugs."

The confinement officer who supervised LBJ in 1971 and 1972 commented on drugs. He believed that no problem existed then within the compound.

LIEUTENANT COLONEL ELI GARDNER: "Drug problems? Hey! Look here. Roughly 45–50 percent of the people who came to the stockade were drug offenders. Now! Everybody says this, but I consider that our searches were so great I think I never found a drug problem inside the stockade. I never found one! The NCOs who worked in that stockade were the best I've ever seen. The Army finally did it. That's the first time I've ever seen a great number of top professionals. Those guys knew what they were doing. I'm talking about [E-] 6s, 7s, 8s [sergeants of various ranks]. A professional bunch. No one can ever swear that nothing ever got in, but those guys kept it down."

Perhaps Gardner was correct, or perhaps he was fooling himself. In any case, if drugs were harder to get inside LBJ during the year he served as confinement officer, it was certainly a turnaround from earlier days.

———

Emboldened by drug use, suffering the torments of withdrawal, psychologically unfit for military service, denying personal responsibility for actions that had brought them to LBJ, feeling "used and abused" by the Green Machine, or acting out their own antisocial attitudes, many prisoners were very hard to control. MPs remembered many such individuals.

GUARD POWERS: "This one guy—a homosexual—they were screwing the hell out of him in the stockade. [We] found out what was going on and put him in maximum security . . . til they could ship him off. Another guy talked in tongues, driving other guys crazy. I happened to be on duty when they brought him in, and he started talking in tongues. The guy on duty with me was a redneck from Texas. 'I can't stand this. This is driving me nuts.' He went down, told him three or four times to shut up. The guy'd quiet down a few minutes and then start up again. Other inmates were complaining, too. "SHUT THAT SONOFABITCH DOWN," they were yelling. So [the guard] went back, smacked him a couple of times. That did it.

"Another guy . . . was in maximum. . . . He'd gotten a Dear John and felt he had nothing left to live for. . . . He sat [in his cell] banging his head against the wall. Boom. Boom. Boom. Must have gone on for forty-five minutes. . . . The next day the guy was gone.

GUARD PROSSER: "Prisoners would go on sick call just to have something to do . . . to break the monotony. One prisoner went just about every day just to have something to make us do . . . . One day he was leaning over on his bunk reading and he got a muscle cramp up through his side into his chest. He thought he was having a heart attack. I called the medic and told him that there was probably nothing wrong . . . . So he . . . talked to the guy and checked him out. . . . He told the guy 'I don't know what's wrong with you but we'll take some blood and test it.' 'You mean you got to stick me?' 'Yeah. We have to analyze it to see what's wrong.'

"He takes blood out of his right arm and puts a cotton ball in his elbow. Then he says, 'We don't know which side of your heart is affected, so we have to take some from your left arm.' Now he's there with cotton balls in both elbows.

"Doc says [to me], 'I'm going to make this guy miserable.' So he gives him an injection with a syringe of cold sugar water right in the butt. Hit him up . . . . His rear end lumped up like a tennis ball and he ricocheted, screaming and hollerin', bouncing right off the walls. Needless to say, we had no more problem with him going on sick call."

Often MPs and their officers faced more difficult inmates, those with an "attitude." One major (later promoted to colonel) who served as deputy to confinement officer Paul Grossheim in 1970–1971, told how difficult it was to work with the inmates.

JAMES PEDERSON: "[An MP] SP-4 received an Article 15 for striking a prisoner, but the prisoner had jumped him first. . . . [On another occasion] a prisoner in DSEG swung a sharpened metal tray at a guard and almost cut off his ear. He reached up, felt his ear, and lost his cool. Went in, struck the prisoner. . . . About the time of the tray incident, a prisoner refused to turn over his tray. . . . The prisoner acted like he was going to fight. We had one guard carry a mattress in, rush the guy, and pin him against the wall. . . . I noticed the guy had a pencil in his right hand and as the guard rushed in, he stepped aside and was only partially caught by the mattress and tried to stab the guard with the pencil. I . . . locked his arm and put my arm around his neck. He bit down on my arm and wouldn't let go. . . . I had to jerk his hair back so we could get his mouth open. . . . Guards had to do the best they could.

"I had urine thrown in my face. [Others] had urine and feces thrown at them."

Others on the staff spoke of the same problems.

GUARD PROSSER: "I had been at [the stockade at] Fort Sill . . . . It was like going from Little League to the majors [when I arrived at LBJ] in terms of the kind of people we were handling. . . . My partner was Ray Boland, from Colorado, an Olympic-caliber college wrestler, but unable to compete in the Olympics because of an injury. We managed to get our hands on a set of weights, and he and I worked out a lot together. We both got pretty big. I was in pretty good shape. There wasn't much else to do. . . . We could take care of ourselves pretty well. That's why they used us there. They referred to us as the Job Squad. We were basically enforcer people. If a prisoner caused trouble we went in a cell and duked it out with him if that was necessary. It was our job. That happened a number of times.

"Because of the climate, the cell block had to be open. It was a screen building on the outside . . . with a walk-around sidewalk. If you were assaulted [through the bars] by a prisoner in a cell [when] you were walking around the block . . . the prisoners on the other side [also] knew what was going on. . . . They couldn't see, but they'd hear and know what was happening and pass the word from cell to cell. . . . You couldn't keep an incident from anybody. We felt at the time that we were pretty vulnerable.

"So if a prisoner was acting up and really causing problems, we felt like enforcement measures had to be taken. I'm not talking about arbitrary beatings. That was something I grew up being taught by my mama, to fight fair. But there were times when I really compromised that. If a prisoner assaulted one of my buddies, I kicked his butt.

"There were times when I had fights with prisoners but I never went in a cell with other guards to gang up on a guy. I had my share of fights because I had my share of assaults. We had things thrown at us, cups of urine thrown on us, but we didn't really have a lot of trouble. I was pretty good at looking ahead of me. I never assumed that nothing was going to happen and kept my eyes on what I was doing and where I was going. More often than not I was pretty well able to dodge most of that stuff. You normally have a pretty good idea of who your troublemakers are and what to expect.

"I *did* have a pretty good altercation with a guy who spit in my sergeant's face one time. Almost on an unspoken order, I took him to the ground and cuffed him and put him in my block. It was not so much a fistfight as a pretty heavy wrestling match.

"[At one point] Ray and I were sent into a cell to remove some contraband. . . . The prisoner swung at me and missed. I swung him around and got him in a headlock and tried to get his arms and subdue him. What I didn't know was that he had made a homemade knife in his cell. Torn apart a butt can, fashioned a blade, wrapped a towel around it for a handle, and sharpened it on the floor. He was just about to stab me in the back when my buddy Ray ran in, knocked up his arm, and grabbed him. The prisoner cut him across the throat, not deep enough to sever the jugular, but hurt him pretty bad."

Prosser was involved in the ear-cutting incident that Colonel Pederson described: "A prisoner . . . swung a chow tray at me through the bars. One of these stainless steel food trays. He missed me. I jumped back, turned around to warn Ray. He was looking down at his key ring and the prisoner, through the bars, hit him in the ear. The corner of the tray went completely through his ear, cut it in half, cut his head really bad under his ear, and almost knocked him out. I tried to go in the cell to subdue the prisoner. The guy had intentionally let his fingernails grow and had sharpened them on the concrete. I was able to pull my head back just in time [but he still] raked my face open from the bottom of my eyelids down to my chin. I had scars for about three years before they faded out. I was lax in this situation because I knew Ray was already hurt, and my response was more emotional than calculated. It was just a real unpleasant assignment. . . . [Many prisoners were] just bad guys. Some judge somewhere probably told them it was a prison or the Army, so they chose the Army.

"We had [this] white prisoner. By talking to him you could tell he was fairly upper-middle class. Ended up in the Army either because he flunked out of college [or] daddy made him join. . . . [E]nded up in Viet Nam, ended up in the stockade because he'd been doing drugs. Claimed to have been doing LSD [and was] really messed up. He was doing all these animal imitations, really acting goofy in his cell. We could pretty much see through it but most of us were not that familiar with the effects of hallucinogens. . . . He was in the cell next to the one where the guy hit Ray with the tray and scratched me pretty bad. When he saw that, he dropped the facade, completely dropped the act, and told us one day, 'Man, I didn't know what you guys went through. I thought it was all a big game. When I saw the guy's ear and your face all clawed up, I felt stupid about what I've been doing.'

"Using a mattress to pin a guy down was also used. This was effective both in terms of less vulnerability to cutting or stabbing weapons and also you can sit on the guy and take your time to figure the best way to get hold of him. We did that a lot. That was about state-of-the-art. There wasn't much else we could do.

"We normally counseled prisoners when we brought them in. . . . [W]e would say, 'Hey, listen, you came in here for a reason. Obviously you're having problems. Don't bring your problems in here or we're going to kick some tail. You behave yourself. You do what you have to do to get out of here. We don't like being here any more than you do. You treat us right, we'll treat you right. Let's just get through this together.' We would try to intimidate them inasmuch as we felt it was beneficial.

"Some of us had been exposed a little bit to behavior modification techniques. We went to a four-week school and were familiar with that. We tried to do some positive reinforcement insofar as we could. There was not a lot of elasticity in that assignment. We'd give them a little more time in the recreation area, be a little more attentive to what they needed, maybe seeing to their needs a little better. We were pretty much locked into a schedule, checking off the prisoners, making sure they were okay, but you could find ways to reinforce better behavior.

"There weren't many black guards [when I was there in 1971]. We had one in maximum security, an E-6 we called Sergeant Rock. A big guy. He was at least as combative, as adversarial, as we were. A career NCO. He was not looked on as a brother by the inmates."

One confinement officer had very strong feelings about both the mission of LBJ and racial problems existing at the time.

LIEUTENANT COLONEL WILLIAM KEYES: "The Army was *so* afraid of a racial situation that they forgot they were dealing with human beings. Black or white doesn't mean diddly-squat. Treat everybody as a human being and everything is going to come out pretty well. Yet they were so afraid that if they did something, people were going to think they were *mean* to blacks. It was ridiculous. Nor did they treat them as soldiers under discipline.

"You've got to understand. They had psychotics in there. These weren't just average black people off the streets; these men were nuts. And they weren't average white people off the streets. These people were much worse to deal with than your average penitentiary inmate. The guy in a penitentiary knows what he's facing and he does his time. These [inmates] were a pretty large group of sociopaths who really came from nowhere and were going nowhere, and this was just a stop in-between for a number of them. . . . As far as I'm concerned, those people were flotsam and jetsam of the world. A professional criminal is at least a professional. The fellows we had were sociopaths with 'be sorry for me' and 'I'm sorry for me' attitudes. . . . When a professional criminal goes [to jail], one of the things he wants to do is cool it with the guards, not be their buddies, but just cool it. These guys wanted to bite down on the bit.

"Blacks were pissed off and 85 percent of the inmates were black. They were being told what a bad situation they had—and in many cases they did—and now they find themselves in Viet Nam and even worse, in LBJ, so now they *know* the Army and entire world has shit on them. As far as they were concerned, they were seeing the absolute truth. A black fellow could end up in LBJ a little easier than a white fellow. That was true. I'm sure the feelings were there."

Reactions of others were even stronger than those expressed by Keyes. Probably most of the white guards were not sympathetic to the new black militancy they saw all around them in American units across southern Viet Nam and even inside the confines of LBJ. One guard may have spoken aloud the opinions held unvoiced by many others.

GUARD MULLIN: "[A]ll those [black] traitors ran around [inside the compound] giving their closed-fist salute. If I had my way, I would have shot them. Unfortunately we lost our ability to command by '68."

Racism. Drugs. Overcrowding. Low morale. Inadequate facilities. Both inmates and staff faced all these problems when Lieutenant Colonel Vernon D. Johnson arrived at Long Binh to take over as confinement officer.

# CHAPTER SIX

# "THEY WERE JUST ANIMALS"

When he took over as confinement officer at the Stockade on 5 July 1968, Lieutenant Colonel Vernon D. Johnson inspected the compound, reviewed LBJ's standing operating procedures, and came to the conclusion that many changes were needed and that they must be made as quickly as possible. He felt confident in his experience and abilities; he was a trained penologist with a Ph.D. Although the previous confinement officer, Lieutenant Colonel George Deringer, and his deputy, Major Norwood Jackson, had listed many projects they had launched to provide work for the prisoners, Johnson noticed an almost total absence of officially approved activities to keep inmates busy, save perhaps for those associated with stockade housekeeping. He began by launching numerous recreational programs: baseball, basketball, softball, weight lifting, and others.

Johnson also felt he understood the psyche of inmates perhaps better than had his predecessors. By listening to them and trying to understand their problems, perhaps by taking action to correct inequities they pointed out, he might ease some of the tensions that threatened to overwhelm his seriously overcrowded facility. To that end he allowed inmates to have more freedom of movement within their respective compounds.

The new confinement officer believed himself to be a fair-minded man, too, and when problems were brought to his attention, he did not automatically assume the accuracy of reports made by guards and staff. Even prisoners had rights, and their status as inmates did not automatically make them liars and scoundrels. Perhaps they had real grievances about the handling they received from guards and staff and, if so, Lieutenant Colonel Johnson wanted to try to set things right. It was no secret to him or anyone else that, in the past, guards sometimes overstepped the boundaries of correct behavior toward their charges. Prisoners had been abused. That would cease under Johnson's watch. Their new confinement officer's attitude did not go over well with those under his command.

Johnson was also greatly concerned over the ease with which prisoners obtained drugs. That also would stop. Only about six weeks after his arrival, on 18 August, Johnson imposed a new rule. All inmates returning from work details or appointments outside the wire would undergo a thorough strip-search to prevent them from smuggling marijuana or other illegal substances into the compound.

This policy, however, set off a reaction that would culminate in disaster. Not only did it create more work for gate guards, but the very inmates Johnson was dedicated to helping reacted powerfully and emotionally. Cut off from their supply of drugs, they experienced deprivation and withdrawal symptoms that heightened their animosity toward all authority figures at LBJ. It was a no-win situation, and calamity loomed ever closer.

Inmates increasingly talked among themselves about the "raw deal" they had received.

_____

Along with Lieutenant Colonel Eugene Murdock, Lieutenant Colonel Herman Trop served at the stockade for a few weeks in the summer of 1968.

LIEUTENANT COLONEL TROP: "The whole stockade was a problem. Morale of prisoners in there was down around zero. I talked to these men and found they had a helluva lot of gripes. They were experiencing a great deal of difficulty: they weren't getting their mail, they weren't getting their pay; they claimed nobody cared about them when they were in their units even when they were hospitalized for wounds. Nobody visited them in the hospital. Some had been tried for cowardice in front of the enemy. This culminated with some fragging their officers."

Prisoners endlessly recycled the wrongs done to them by their fellows, their units, officers at their courts-martial who adjudged them guilty, and the Army itself. They were innocent. They had been preyed on because of matters outside their control, and now they suffered the injustice of being locked up at LBJ. Of all the former inmates interviewed for this book, only one ever admitted that he might have been sent into confinement for good and proper reasons. All the rest simply poured out their resentment of what had happened to them. Here are some of their stories, beginning with the man who accepted the fact that he was imprisoned for breaking the rules, although he did so because he believed that the rules were wrong. He was incarcerated at LBJ in 1967 when it was still being built at Long Binh.

INMATE PRIVATE ANDREW HUDAK: "I was assigned to the 23rd of the 25th Infantry Division northwest of Saigon. A heliborne operation was planned for a late Saturday night or early Sunday morning in November 1966. I was twenty-eight at the time. I refused to go. I wanted to do something against this war, so I refused the order. I was naive, thinking I would be listened to. I was laughed at. I was convicted of refusing a direct order, and they gave me five years . . . but with abatement time, they kept cutting the time down. . . . I did what I did all on my own. The whole intent was to work against war. I don't want us to be taken over by the military way of thinking.

"For the first time ever I was in a stockade. . . . This couldn't be happening to me. . . . I got along pretty well with guards. . . . They were exceptional. They would go out of their way. . . . It was the fellow convicts you had to watch. . . . There were a lot of drugs at LBJ. That was one of the main reasons to stay away from everyone. . . . I guess most of the people in the confinement area belonged there. They had done some crime or other. Some were there because they had made a mistake. They were nice guys. . . . You always find people in common . . . so you get a group of guys kind of like yourself. . . . We played a lot of chess, Monopoly, did a lot of talking, read a lot.

Most of the time I worked as a KP [kitchen police], sometimes outside the fence with a guard."

Others who told their stories were less objective than Hudak or at least strongly believed they were not responsible for their situations. However misguided, these beliefs were genuine.

INMATE PRIVATE GREGG PAYTON: "I was nineteen years old, an urban American from Jersey City. I had never been away from home. I was in a supply unit at MACV headquarters. . . . I was sent [to LBJ] for AWOL, assault, disrespect for an officer, misappropriation of government funds. I had three court-martials. . . . A lot of times I was in a fog.

"We were confronted with a lot of situations in Viet Nam, primarily racism. . . . [W]hen I began to see what was going on, I began to talk about the racism issues. Black GIs in my unit constantly caught all the dirty details. . . . [I] began to say I didn't care to be involved in this war. People began to carry resentments against me. My life was threatened on occasions; I got beat up one time. . . . I had gotten very despondent. I was working on some way of defecting when I was picked up as an AWOL near Camp David in Saigon."

Payton believed that it was racism that had brought him to LBJ. It was so easy an answer. He seems not to have realized that no matter his color, going AWOL, assaulting another man, showing disrespect to an officer, and misappropriating funds were all legitimate court-martial offenses, two of which would also have brought felony charges in civilian life. It was easier and it better protected his psyche to blame his misfortunes on racism.

INMATE PRIVATE JAMES B. VAUGHAN: "[While I was at LBJ] they took me over to the 24th Evac[uation Hospital] emergency room and I went in there and they told me to 'Sit down. Just sit down.' And from way across the room this voice rang out which was the prettiest voice in the whole world. It was this medic I had served with between Chu Lai and Da Nang when I worked out in the field. He said (I'm fixin' to start crying. Excuse me.) 'Take those handcuffs off him.' It was so much of a catharsis to see him. The first friendly face I had seen in—I mean these sons of bitches are trying to put me away for *life* over nothing.

"When I went to the stockade [for pretrial confinement], a lot of the guys in my unit stole all the evidence. [My officers] wanted to send me to jail. So [now] they couldn't court-martial me. . . . They treated me like poison when I went back [from LBJ] to my unit. Wanted to scare me into . . . taking an undesirable [discharge]. I finally found out that all the evidence [against me] was missing. One day the First Sergeant came down and said, 'They're going to offer you a Article 15'. . . . It was a lieutenant colonel who was giving me a field grade Article 15. . . . They had all these charges and asked me how I pled. I told them I pled not guilty. They said, 'You son of a bitch, you're guilty.' And the lieutenant colonel said, 'You're busted from E-3 to E-1,' and fined me $100. For that I spent forty-two days in max and like to got raped and I still have nightmares about it.

"So I said, 'That's bullshit doing that to me. Where's your proof? If you had any, you'd be giving me a damn general court-martial'. . . . There were all these captains and lieutenants in there . . . . He snatched the Article 15 up like he was going to send me back to the stockade, and I said, 'You can't do it. I know it and you know it. You're just try-ing to scare me, but I'll go ahead and sign this piece of junk because all I want is to get out of this chicken shit Army and go home.' I liter-ally jerked the piece of paper out of his hand. I didn't want to be out there burning shit, being a shit-burner. About the next day I got orders to go to Camp Alpha, which was the processing center at Bien Hoa to get your ass home."

INMATE PRIVATE RUDOLPH GRAY: "I was In-Country from June 1967 to 13 July 1969. . . . I was assigned to the 86th Transporta-tion Company and was a light and heavy vehicle driver, a good one. I was eighteen. When I first got over there the people looked funny. Little short people. The place stunk. There were big bumblebees. Good grief! Mosquitoes were 'mosquatos' they were so big. How come insects were so big and the people was so small? . . . I was stockade-bound as soon as I got there! . . . I was on convoy duty. Out of nowhere one day while we was lined up comes a five-ton tractor and it rams me. I'm parked; haven't moved yet. I signed the accident report. Three weeks later, the captain pulls the record and gives me an Article 15. I was busted to lowest grade, given two weeks of extra duty, took part of my pay, and was grounded. They couldn't get any soldiering out of me after that.

"I got sent to LBJ the first time for shooting my rifle on New Year's, January 1968. I was gambling, went broke, so got up and went outside with my rifle and started shooting it off. Shit. There were thousands of guys in Vietnam shooting their rifles and they arrested me. I got thirty days inside LBJ for that.

"After I got out . . . they transferred me to [another] transportation company, about ten miles northeast of Saigon . . . but they wouldn't let me drive. Don't give Gray his weapon, they say, for he's a hazard to officers. I told them if they keep messin' with me, I'd kill 'em. That was dumb to say . . . . They made me a permanent guard. I said I wouldn't pull guard duty no more. I put in to go back to driving. . . . They put me up on a tower, so I went up there and laid down. There was an important inspection and they looked up and couldn't see me and said I was sleeping, but I wasn't.

"I was working guard duty with a guy . . . out of Detroit. We were pullin' two hours on, four hours off. [While I was asleep] he left post, don't tell me nothing. The sergeant of the guard comes around, finds me asleep. 'Why aren't you on guard?' 'The other guy is on duty,' I say. But he wasn't. He gone. So I get busted.

"My eleven months in Nam were up. I DEROSed [back to the States]. I came as an E-1, I left as an E-1. Went back to the States and was assigned to Fort Hood, Texas, for less than a month. I volunteered for Viet Nam and was assigned to the 534th Transportation Company at Long Binh.

"Something happened. They sent me to make a convoy drive of about seventy-five miles from Long Binh to Quan Loi. . . . I said okay if they'd give me a convoy to Vung Tau afterwards. Vung Tau was an R & R [rest and recreation] center. I went to Quan Loi and got back on a Friday. I was asleep. They woke me up and said, 'Gray, you're on convoy to Quan Loi again.' 'No, I'm not!' 'Yes, you are.' All hell broke out. . . . I jumped on the sergeant. Two more joined in. Sent me back to quarters. I took a bunch of pills, Binoctals. They're for migraine headaches, have about six or seven hundred milligrams. I took about eight. Tried to commit suicide. They revived me. Two days later I was in the stockade. The court gave me six months and reduced me to E-1 [again]. I was in LBJ for forty-eight days, from 24 May to 10 July 1969."

One of the earlier prisoners was a U.S. Navy man, Charles Kries. After arriving in Viet Nam he tired of military life and went absent without leave.

CHARLES KRIES: "I went AWOL in Saigon [in 1968], but didn't do much hiding. I was out and about all the time. I was gone about 300 days before the MPs picked me up. I was caught during a black market money exchange. [When I arrived at LBJ] they would not let me wear my Navy dungarees, they made me wear Army fatigues. My first two weeks was spent in the Tiger Cages . . . . My stay was thirty-three days. . . . We were not allowed to make noise at any time, but made animal noises like dogs, chickens, and horses to harass the guards. . . . There was nothing to do. We just *sat!* . . . The guards were rough. Shouted. Hit. Beat some. They'd go into a cubicle, throw a blanket over a guy and beat the shit out of him. . . . They didn't treat Americans like Americans should be treated. Some guards were ass-holes. One day a guard called out my name while we were in for-mation. He mispronounced my name like 'crys.' I corrected him. 'Krees, sir,' I said. The guard brought me up on charges of being insubordinate."

Lieutenant Colonel Willam Keyes, confinement officer from November 1968 to November 1969 during Kries's stay at LBJ, reacted to this tale.

WILLIAM KEYES: "That's a story. That's a real story, because to be brought up on punishment he'd have to be brought before me and somebody brought up on a charge of correcting a sergeant's mispronunciation of his name? As far as beatings were concerned, I can only say that I don't know what happens at two o'clock in the morning when I'm asleep. On the other hand, people knew what would happen if I caught them. I'd court-martial them. No question about that.

"Stories get magnified, over the years, in the telling. *If* there were rampant beatings going on, I would have known. . . . Stories change. I become braver. As a kid I jumped on a firecracker. No, it wasn't a firecracker, it was a hand grenade. No, it wasn't a hand grenade. It was a bomb."

INMATE PRIVATE JEREMIAH JAMES: "I was only nineteen or twenty . . . in the field down in the Delta with my unit . . . .We were in the rice paddies. The unit had moved out of its base camp after Tet and had set up a new camp in a bad place. All it was was a perimeter, wooded on all sides. We took an extraordinary amount of sniper fire. We never know where it comes from. It went on days and weeks. My nerves became uneasy. I was hot, no showers, nothing clean. Jumping at anything. I was tired of not knowing when I was going to die. I was clean out of my head. I was seeing VC for looking so hard for 'em. I couldn't tell anybody how I was feeling for it wouldn't be manly. We were short on men, too. Only the most seriously wounded was rotated out. Others were kept there until their DEROS. I was busy trying to figure why I was killin' folk. There was this incident in which my lieutenant threw a white phosphorus grenade on a little girl. By her size she was somewhere between three and six. . . . Then I mistook some of my own men for VC and shot at 'em. Nobody was hurt. . . . I was out of it. The next day I got an M-16 and wanted to take my own life.

"I got into it with [this] sergeant . . . because I wasn't wearing my steel pot. . . . It was too hot and I said I didn't want to wear it. . . . He hit me, but I never hit him. The first sergeant saw this, thought we was fighting and he brought charges up against me. I was confined from 7 June to 19 July [at USARVIS] on those charges, then I was tried on the nineteenth and I pled guilty. They reduced me to E-1, forfeited pay and privileges, given fourteen years and a dishonorable discharge. I was put back in LBJ to await a stateside transfer to Fort Leavenworth."

Although James may have been unaware of the fact, it was his sergeant's responsibility to insure his men protected themselves from enemy fire as well as possible, and this included wearing helmets. Who knew at what moment an unseen sniper might fire a round at some unsuspecting U.S. soldier? James seems to have believed

An aerial view of Long Binh Jail (just below center) prior to 1968.
*Courtesy of the U.S. Army*

*All photographs courtesy of Paul Grossheim unless noted otherwise*

The chapel at the old LBJ.
*Courtesy of Vernon Swim*

A guard tower rises above the fence line.
*Courtesy of Vernon Swim*

Guard searching prisoners at the gate to the pre-trial compound.

Lieutenant Colonel George C. Deringer and Major Norwood Jackson at LBJ in June 1968.

The latrine and shower facilities.

The minimum-custody barracks.

Parolees marching.

Under guard, new prisoners are escorted to the reception area.

Prisoners filling sandbags in the "Big Red" work area.

Prisoners making aircraft security blocks.

Guards checking out an inmate leaving the stockade.

The newly constructed maximum-security area.

Chaplain Wayne King holding a chapel service.

Meal time at the mess hall.

Chaplain Vernon Swim in front of the officers' quarters.
*Courtesy of Vernon Swim*

Chaplain Wayne King, Specialist Dennis Hensley, and Chaplain Vernon Swim. Hensley, a chaplain's assistant, was reassigned from LBJ for writing a story about the stockade that appeared in *Overseas Weekly*.
*Courtesy of Vernon Swim.*

Conex shipping containers made into maximum-security cells.

Watchtower along the line of double fence wire surrounding the prison.

An armed guard in an LBJ watchtower.

his sergeant was being "mean" to him by insisting that he wear his helmet.

Already sentenced to LBJ by circumstances beyond their control, inmates regularly claimed that life inside the compound was hell itself. Their treatment at the stockade was beyond belief. It did not matter whether a staff member was black or white; all of them were supposedly out to brutalize inmates as savagely and as often as possible.

INMATE PRIVATE GERALD STOVALL: "A lot of people in power who ran the stockade were black and the prisoners couldn't understand how they could treat their own people the way they were treatin' them. They treated us worse than the white guards did. They always had to show the white man that 'all of us are not like that.' They feel this desire to be accepted. The only way to prove they're not like us is to put the hard screws to us."

INMATE PRIVATE GREGG PAYTON: "[A] guard . . . from Baltimore? A black man? Every black prisoner hated him; he did a lot of foul stuff. I don't know if he's still living because I know a lot of guys who were serious about going back and eliminating him. I could see about fifteen guys stabbing him in the heart. He hid behind his badge and authority. He saw to it that people went to the box, harassed people. He was in charge of Big Red. Sandbag quotas. A slave situation. He wouldn't give anybody any slack. No kind of compassion in the guy. He created a lot of pain in me."

INMATE PRIVATE GERALD STOVALL: "Most of the guards who worked there had a little sadism in them, I would say. . . . I had to go to court to be tried on my AWOL charge. While I was doing that I got high on Binoctals. By the time I got back to the stockade, I'm ripped. Instead of carrying me to my hooch, they put me in The Box. When I got there, they said I was moving too slow and commenced to jump on me and beat me up. The next morning . . . when they knocked on my door I told them to go to hell; I'm not aware of where I am right now. They guy behind me shouted to . . . do what they wanted. 'They just beat you up last night,' he said. When I came out of my cell I walked past a mirror. I saw how my face was all swollen, but I never got any medical treatment for that. Hey! I'm not an idiot, so I did what they say.

"[At one point] this black guard was dragging 'Baby San'— seventeen or eighteen years old—down toward the conexes and beatin' him.[1] He threw Baby San up in the conex and . . . and the guard couldn't get in there so he went and got some tear gas canisters and threw those in the cell. I was in the next conex and had a chance to see the guard up close. . . . [W]hen I looked at his face, it was the closest thing I have ever seen to a devil. His eyes. He'd jumped on Baby San because Baby San asked him, 'How come you're doin' this to a brother?' That triggered him off. He was about 6´5˝, slim but big, very big lips, big droopy eyes, a big thick mustache, a medium brown complexion, very long arms. . . . I think I heard he works as a guard for the D.C. Department of Corrections now."

Even one of the staff members confirmed some of the complaints made by prisoners. He worked in the supply office and presumably had opportunity to observe his surroundings.

KEN COWAN: "People are human. The guards were frustrated with being in Vietnam. They were frustrated because their wives were playing around on them. Their girlfriends left them. They have to work twelve hours a day. Half the prisoners were animals who came through there from being out in the field so long they don't give a shit about life. They're threatening you. . . .

"In the old LBJ they had MP guys working in maximum security who were really just animals. These guys would beat the crap out of you when you first got there. Attitude adjustment. . . . Right inside the main gate. They'd have you strip down and wait for you to say something wrong and then they'd just beat the crap out of you. . . . I didn't like them and I can get along with anybody. They pretty much lived just to go in and beat the crap out of somebody. Oh gosh, yes, I saw it. It pretty much scared me. This guy's going to come unglued and come after me! 'You don't have to hit this guy. He wasn't making any big trouble. He just wanted to go take a leak.' 'He doesn't need to take a leak,' and he'd jab him with his nightstick. And I had to see

---

[1]Probably given this nickname because of his use of Binoctals, often known as "Number 10" or "Baby San Number Ten."

these guys at the end of the day in the company area. I heard about it happening a lot of times and seen it happen a couple of times.

"This was in the old part when I first got there. . . . One of the MPs treated me okay, but he was a flat animal. Put a chain on this guy! Unbelievable! . . . They had to be reprimanded quite a few times before they finally slowed up. . . . It was so hush-hush. . . . You couldn't talk about anything that was happening inside at all. . . . If you got caught at *anything*, you were out of there in a second! Dennis Hensley, for example, who was a chaplain's assistant, got thrown out for writing a nice article about the place. There was nothing wrong with what he said. But he was gone."

Another man at LBJ, a guard, generally agreed with Cowan.

PRIVATE FIRST CLASS THOMAS MCKEON: "[T]here was a lot of brutality. In the jail guards saw all the inmates the same, in a bad light, plus they took it out on them because of what they were charged with. [A] lot of blacks were killing white lifer squad leaders to get out of the field. . . . but then they had to deal with the guards when they got to the jail."

Not surprisingly, few others who served at LBJ agreed with Cowan or McKeon. Most officers and men of the custodial staff had different memories. They recalled using force, warranted force, they believed, to control inmates only when they acted up. But brutality? They were not guilty of that. Nor would force of any kind have been necessary had inmates only followed the rules set forth to govern their behavior.

One lieutenant colonel who served at LBJ during a particularly crucial time testified at an investigative hearing that the biggest problem facing the staff was the kind of inmate held there.

MP LIEUTENANT COLONEL IVAN NELSON: "The guards are under tremendous pressure all the time. . . . [A] prisoner told one of my officers that when he got out of the stockade, he would find the officer's wife, rape her, and then kill her. I have never been exposed to the type of prisoners we have here now. The prisoners here are not like the ones in the States. . . . [H]ere a released prisoner may have to return to the battlefield and may be subsequently killed. Most . . . feel they have been misused, and they want to get even by hurting someone or destroying something."

As for rampant brutality, one confinement officer simply dis-
believed that it had ever been a real problem.

LIEUTENANT COLONEL WILLIAM KEYES: "Prisoners are
liars. They have to be, for their only shot at self-respect is to lie so
often they can convince themselves. They lie about everything."

Keyes's conclusion was echoed by other officers.

COLONEL JAMES PEDERSON: "During the four or five months
I was there in 1966 and '67, I can honestly say I knew of no case
where a guard brutalized a prisoner. . . . [A] black guard [during my
second tour in 1970 and 1971] was given punishment for striking a
prisoner. . . . There were some rumors about him and finally one of
the other guards did see him strike another prisoner. He was pulled
out, given punishment, and became a driver.

"I do not recall any incident where we were able to prove there
was brutality. . . . [W]e just couldn't prove it. Some prisoners complained, but in each case we found that the prisoner was dreaming it
up to get a guard in trouble because that guard was making him toe
the line. I'm not blind to the fact that some incidents did actually
take place.

"The guards had to put up with a lot. I don't deny that maybe
some things happened, but I believe if they did, they were rare. Now
I know that NCOs live in their own world and often keep knowledge
of things from their officers, but I was vigilant. . . . Sometimes when
prisoners couldn't manipulate a guard, they'd register complaints
about him so as to get him moved.

"I was able to prove against a couple of [staff] NCOs that they
were verbally abusive; they antagonized the prisoners. We moved
them . . . out of the stockade even though it was hard to find NCOs
[who wanted to work there].

"During my first tour we did have some NCOs who came in from
Infantry units who had physical profiles because of injuries. We *did*
have trouble with some of them. They didn't want to be there to start
with. . . . We had to run off some of them [who had] very, very negative attitudes against the prisoners, thought they were scum and
talked to them as if they were."

A Judge Advocate General officer also denied that prisoners were badly mistreated.

CAPTAIN BEN YUDESIS: "I suspect that inmates who speak of brutality . . . are just putting out 'convict talk.' This is an old prosecutor *and* defense counselor talking. There were probably some incidents where somebody got punched around, but probably very little of it. . . . I think the treatment was straightforward. . . . We conducted investigations where some guys claimed to have been assaulted and basically found that in one or two instances they had been struck. But that was because they had assaulted a guard and their bruises were a result of having been restrained, and that was primarily in the maximum security section."

GUARD SERGEANT SAM MULLIN: "I have beaten prisoners. Okay? I have beaten him til I got him off his feet and pinned down and manacled. Usually the beating consisted of throwing him into a judotype lock and onto the ground. I *never* knowingly punched a guy in the eye. I have knowingly punched him in the gut or elbowed him to take the wind out of him. . . . I know every NCO who worked in that jail in '66, '67, '68 and they wouldn't tolerate that. . . . We knew we could drive a mile to the highway, take a left, drive down . . . and get a cool Coke and a blow-job for fifty piasters and come back. We could put up with their shit for a month because we knew they couldn't do that."

One confinement officer acknowledged the seriousness of the morale problems at LBJ.

LIEUTENANT COLONEL WILLIAM KEYES: "The attitude among both personnel and prisoners was bad. As a matter of fact, I had one sergeant guard who wasn't too bright who told me how he didn't believe in beating inmates like some guys. He would take them into the latrine, take the head off the shower and shove their face up there into the water until they started choking and then they were good boys after that. I got rid of him."

That guard, however, was not alone. For years those midnight showers were a way guards dealt with inmates, sometimes on an almost casual basis. Many prisoners remembered either being subjected to them or hearing of others who were forcibly held under the water stream while desperately trying to breathe.

Chaplains also commented about inmates' charges of brutality.

CHAPLAIN VERNON SWIM: "I never heard of any physical abuse by the guards. I know they tended to look on prisoners as animals, although we tried to work on the guards' attitude. Prisoners made themselves obnoxious to the staff sometimes. . . . That was an element we had to continue to work on with the guards."

CHAPLAIN WAYNE KING: "Brutality? When Colonel Grossheim was the commander, there was no brutality. The inmates may have perceived that some stuff done was brutality. For instance, if you want to move somebody from one cell to the next and he doesn't want to move, it looks like there's brutality if you're watching. Take a mattress, open the door, pin the guy against the far wall with the mattress. The guards are the ones who get hurt in these things, not the inmates."

The stories differ. Inmates stress mistreatment. Officials deny it happened. Even if brutality did occur, it did not always run just one way. Nor did one have to be a guard to be in danger.

CLERK KEN COWAN: "[While I worked in the supply office] I got hurt once. I got stabbed with a ball point pen between my first and second fingers. I still have about a ¾″ scar from it. I was handing out mail, and this guy said, 'Hey, you're late with my mail, you so-and-so.' I gave him his mail between the bars, and he has this pen and he stabs me."

After reading accounts from both groups, the question remains open. Were the stories about brutality, willful mistreatment of inmates, true, or were they the stuff of prison legend? A partial and perhaps final answer to that question comes from the records of the Army itself, not declassified until 3 May 1990, seventeen years after the last combat soldier came home from Viet Nam.

In the fall of 1968, David Miller, Saigon bureau chief of the Columbia Broadcasting System (CBS), asked for permission from USARV Headquarters to investigate allegations of brutality at LBJ. Not surprisingly, his request was denied. His interest in the matter did, however, bestir Army officials to look into the matter themselves, and the USARV chief of staff directed its Office of Inspector General (IG) to conduct an investigation. That directive came down on 12 January 1969. Six officers assigned to the IG office did their work quickly between 13 January and 21 January. On 17 February 1969 the chief of staff approved their "findings and recommendations."

The IG looked into twenty-one alleged cases of brutality and/or prisoner mistreatment dating from 1 September 1968 to 13 January 1969. His office investigated complaints that prisoners were hit and beaten by guards, and that guards harassed prisoners in both DSEG and the medium security compound. The IG final report stated: "Four guards testified that on at least one occasion each had hit a prisoner or saw another guard hit a prisoner. . . . There was provocation in each case, but the fact remains that, contrary to regulations, prisoners were hit."

Most of the investigated beatings occurred during the month of November 1968 or earlier and took place inside the compound supervisor's office located in the conex area, a closed building with no way for outsiders to observe what was happening within. As a result of the investigation, that office was remodeled into a more open area, as also were latrines, showers, and other similar areas.

On 14 January 1969, a former confinement officer, Lieutenant Colonel Ivan Nelson, gave testimony to the IG of what he had done to prevent further abuses.

IVAN NELSON: "I have suspected from time to time that prisoners have been maltreated. In all [such] instances . . . the USARV Inspector General inquired into the matter. In one instance . . . I relieved one NCO from duty with this stockade. . . . In addition I have opened up the sides of all latrines, showers, compound offices, and barber shop so that there is no place a prisoner can be taken where acts of brutality or maltreatment by cadremen or prisoners cannot be observed. . . . On three or four occasions I have suspected that incidents were not what they appeared to be on the surface. On such occasions I have rotated cadre among the compounds. This seems to work."

Consequently, in the months toward the end of the period in question, the final IG report stated, "tension has subsided and the number and frequency of altercations involving prisoners and guards have decreased. Many possible witnesses had returned to CONUS and therefore were unavailable to give testimony. Guards could not remember prisoners' names who alleged mistreatment. Inmates could not recall the names of guards or specific circumstances."

Two physicians, Captain Ronald L. Zerby and Captain Benson Seliksky, appeared before the IG and stated that three men they treated "were beaten by someone in the stockade." Lieutenant Colonel Smith of the IG office observed one prisoner in his cell on the day of a reported incident and noted that the inmate's "face, lips and eyes were swollen and there were other bruises that in all probability resulted from being hit. . . . rather than being restrained as alleged by the guards." The investigating team concluded that "possibly all three prisoners were injured in the process of being subdued or restrained. There was no evidence to indicate deliberate beatings or brutality toward the prisoners."

One prisoner, J. Newkirk, spoke to the IG about the infamous water treatments long used at LBJ. Used by guards as a punitive measure, these consisted of taking a prisoner into a shower, pinching his nose closed while holding his head back, and allowing water to run into his mouth until he gagged. Newkirk alleged that about 23 December 1968 he was handcuffed and taken to the shower by five guards. "They held my head under the shower for about two minutes and when I'd pull back to breathe, they beat me on the chest and stomach. This lasted for about 10 minutes, during which I was knocked to the floor twice." Many other prisoners told similar stories. An MP guard private first class corroborated their tales. "You hold their head back and put them under the full force of the shower. Actually you get as wet as they do but they get a mouth full of water. I really don't know if it's legal but we don't do it unless the supervisor authorizes it. When I first came here we did [it] but we don't do it much now." Most guards dismissed such incidents, claiming either that they had never heard of such an act or that showers were used for hygienic purposes, reserved for inmates who refused to shower or who had urinated and/or defecated on themselves and needed to be cleaned up. The IG inspectors determined that "the water treatment was administered as a form of punishment and constitutes a form of maltreatment of prisoners."

Prisoners had also alleged harassment in the maximum security area. The IG report noted that in DSEG conexes the canvas cots were removed from the boxes daily at 4 A.M., and prisoners then had "no place to sit except the floor of the CONEX," and concluded that "Overall conditions in the CONEX area are the least desirable in the stockade. The area is established to administratively segregate prisoners who by their conduct and attitude tend to disrupt normal prison routine when allowed to mingle with other prisoners. The controls are stringent, privileges restrictive and living conditions austere. These measures are not meant to harass, but to deter and control trouble makers."

Other prisoners had maintained that harassment also extended to the medium security compound. Several of those complaints are worth repeating, the first primarily because it sounds like the plaint of a whining boy:

—"they make you count cadence real loud . . . . I am real hoarse and that yelling hurts my throat."

—"they throw prisoners in the CONEX's for the least little thing."

—"There is constant harassment here until you can't do anything right."

—"You think you are doing right and the next thing you are in the CONEX. You just don't know what to do."

—"A guard whose name I don't know said I cursed him."

—"They are always making men do push-ups and swearing at them. A couple of days ago a prisoner . . . was made to do push-ups all day long."

—"They just wear you down . . . unless you kiss the guards' asses."

—"This stockade is not fair but firm—you are required to do push-ups for no reason at all."

The IG report concluded that "The general allegation of harassment cannot be substantiated. . . . Those confined . . . are the prisoners who have, by their attitude or actions, demonstrated an unwillingness to abide by the prison regulations. . . . The prison population . . .

includes approximately 35.5% second offenders . . . . Many of these have used . . . drugs. They are aggressive and belligerent. Accordingly firm, positive means must be used to prevent these troublemakers from succeeding in their efforts to disrupt normal prison routine. . . . [P]risoners . . . continue to challenge authority at every opportunity. . . . The comparatively few incidents . . . is indicative of successful self control by custodial personnel and belie the idea of deliberate maltreatment and brutality.

"Prisoners [have] continued for months to challenge the authority of guards at every opportunity. Guards were cursed, assaulted and generally harassed. In such an environment custodial personnel have erred and minor excesses were used. . . . There is a decided lack of written instructions promulgated to stockade custodial personnel regarding policies and procedures. This lack is seriously hampering uniformity of operations and complete understanding of what is required and expected. . . . There is . . . a decided lack of an organized and formal training program for the lower grade enlisted custodial personnel."

As a result of the final report, one sergeant first class was transferred "to duties not connected with the operation of the USARV stockade," and a blanket prohibition was laid down preventing further use of the "water treatment" method of disciplining inmates.

This Army investigation and its subsequent IG report came too late. All the troubles noted in the final report and others uninvestigated—low morale of both staff and inmates, a facility seething with racism, vengeful prisoners representing some of the worse of antisocial tendencies, an understrength staff and overcrowded compounds, too lax control of inmates, resentment for real or imagined mistreatment—came down on the head of Lieutenant Colonel Vernon Johnson just fifty-five days after he took over command of the Long Binh stockade compound. His time had run out. On the night of 29 August 1968 rioting broke out within the wire surrounding LBJ. Before morning, Johnson lay on the ground inside the compound, so grievously wounded by desperate inmates determined to wreak havoc that he would soon be invalided out of the service. Other men would have to pick up the pieces.

By that same date, former confinement officer Lieutenant Colonel George Deringer, Johnson's predecessor, had moved on to a new assignment. No longer in Viet Nam, he served as provost marshal at Fort McArthur, California. In a letter drafted years after the event, he set forth his reactions to the news from LBJ.

GEORGE DERINGER: "I was surprised—shocked—and surely disappointed when I learned of the riot . . . when the news reached me. I was listening to a radio at my desk when the announcement came out which I [incorrectly] interpreted as 'RIOT AT LONG BEACH.' I called in the Sergeant Major and asked if there was a stockade at Long Beach Naval Station. He responded, 'Col, if you're talking about the riot—it occurred at the LBJ-Viet Nam.' I about fell out of my chair!!!

"The sudden departure of myself and Major Jackson did not make Lieutenant Colonel Johnson's task an easy one. He stepped in during a period of high intensity in all of Viet Nam. Just what he did or didn't do I'll never be privy to but somehow—something occurred over there that set that thing off. I've searched my soul many many times trying to cipher out my activities, etc., and—from the way I see—there's nothing my administration did—or didn't do to plant the seed. The fault may never be known."

# CHAPTER SEVEN

# "KILL THE CHUCKS"

Some of the more militant blacks imprisoned at LBJ during 1967 and 1968 came to believe that the conditions of their imprisonment were absolutely intolerable. A Judge Advocate General Corps officer, Colonel Herbert Green, a man who would later preside over courts-martial of several of them, gave some small support for their complaints.

COLONEL GREEN: ". . . it was terribly overcrowded. . . . Commanders could place soldiers into pretrial confinement without a neutral magistrate's review. In too many instances commanders abused pretrial confinement and incarcerated many soldiers when pretrial confinement was not appropriate.

"The general operating policy was that unless a soldier was punitively discharged [as a result of his court-martial] his sentence was served in the stockade. As a result there were many prisoners in the stockade who were serving their full terms. Another group . . . were those pending shipment to . . . stateside confinement facilities. These . . . prisoners greatly exceeded the proper capacity. Thus there was in one relatively small area a large number of criminals, a substantial portion of whom were violent, antisocial individuals. Added to that was the hot weather, which often makes one irritable, and lack of facilities to keep the prisoners productive and busy. . . . [T]his combination was deadly and probably made the riot inevitable.

"[It] was not a particularly pleasant place but not that much worse than living conditions experienced by a number of our soldiers stationed in Viet Nam. . . . I did not believe that the stockade was a hell hole where prisoners were systematically and regularly tortured. . . . [I]t was basically a holding area for criminals.

"Every entering prisoner . . . was required to spend two weeks in a segregated area composed of CONEX containers. . . . This was mandated to get the prisoners' attention . . . . [T]here was no legal justification for [it]. . . . [T]his was essentially mass punishment for pretrial prisoners who should not be punished prior to trial. The presumption of innocence was systematically ignored. Also ignored was Article 13 of the Uniform Code of Military Justice, which prohibits pretrial restraint any more rigorous than that necessary to insure the presence of the accused for trial."

Colonel Green thus makes plain that some rights of those sent to LBJ were abused. That was the case, however, uniformly for all, black or white. What all too many of those inmates at LBJ serving the sentences mandated by their courts-martial ignored was the fact that they had become convicted criminals. They had broken one or another of the military laws that governed their behavior and they were now suffering the consequences of those acts. For most of them, had they been in civilian life rather than under military law, they would still have been incarcerated for their deeds. It was not the Army that had done them wrong. They had done it to themselves. Now they were inmates at LBJ. The Army did not send criminals to prison so they could enjoy the good life. As lawbreakers, these men should have expected hard work, unpleasant quarters, and institutional food. Sweeping the dirt of the compound over and again and filling sandbags were not activities that qualified as unconstitutional slave labor. Living in tents raised on floorboards and sometimes being held in conex boxes was not cruelty.

Yet as 1968 wore on, a small group of blacks and possibly a very few trusted whites began to make escape plans. Their lives at LBJ, they believed, were so unpleasant that they could no longer endure them. These men had been planning to break out of LBJ for some time. They would free themselves and anyone else who wanted to join them.

Perhaps they were influenced by the popular 1963 movie *The*

*Great Escape,* starring Steve McQueen, that told the story of an escape from a German prisoner-of-war camp. They also knew how the Viet Cong had honeycombed the land with tunnels. For whatever reason, they decided to dig a tunnel under the compounds, beneath the wire, continue it for a distance outside and then burrow up to the surface. Escape would be under covering darkness. Once outside LBJ, they would head for Ha Noi where they would ask the North Vietnamese for sanctuary in return for renouncing America, the U.S. Army and its policies in Viet Nam.

One inmate who was involved remembered the plans for an escape and how they were betrayed.

INMATE PRIVATE GERALD STOVALL: "We had holes dug all over the compound. Tunnels . . . we'd dug in trying to escape. We had a tunnel dug all the way from our hooch clear through to the back fence. Everybody that be in Viet Nam know about tunnels. A lot of the guys in LBJ had been tunnel rats. We had dug this tunnel. We were ready to go and one of the guys who had a long sentence waiting to go to Leavenworth ended up snitching us all. So that's how they found out about that tunnel. We were supposed to leave like that next night. He talked everybody into waitin' and while everybody was waitin' he went and told on us. All the way out under the fence and up under the guard post."

INMATE PRIVATE NATHANIEL FORT JR.: "I got in with some guys who were trying to escape . . . . They had planned to go to Ha Noi. Lot of guys in there felt they got the shaft just like I did and wanted no part of the United States or the government. . . . We had discussed that quite a few times and planned it. . . . A lot of guys. I found out because I was put in the barracks with those guys. I guess they found I was okay and included me. . . . Seems like half the barracks was in the thing. . . . How were we going to get out? In Viet Nam they got a lot of tunnels . . . and we were going to try to go underground. . . . hit a water drain or something. That was the route we were goin' to take. It wasn't goin' over any walls. . . . But somebody in there was a snitch and went back and told . . . . Matter of fact, the night we was going to escape, they found out and locked us all up in maximum security."

These efforts at tunneling were thus known to the authorities at LBJ. A confinement officer downplayed any possibility of success.

LIEUTENANT COLONEL EUGENE MURDOCK: "The inmates were working on a tunnel they thought was secret. It went from medium compound out toward the fence. We knew right where they were all the time. Oh, yeah. One of those damn [Army] engineers had a sensor there. Yeah, hell. [laughs] 'They're getting closer.' It gave them something to do. Yeah. Really."

He might not have been so sanguine had he known the extent of the digging.

Even after the riot some inmates refused to give up on the idea that they might be able to tunnel their way out of the prison and escape to the North. On 11 September 1968, following the riot, Sergeant First Class Theodore R. Logan of the 284th MP Company testified to investigators what he had discovered the day before at about 8:15 A.M. as he was walking through Sentenced Compound A while gathering prisoners for a work detail.

GUARD LOGAN: "I noticed a considerable amount of dirt banked up in the area of the tent nearest the perimeter fence. An empty fifty gallon drum was lying down in a recess in the ground. Upon closer inspection I saw a large hole under the drum. Suspecting that it was a tunnel I returned to the gate leading to the Admin area and informed Major Williams of what I had found. Major Williams told me to check it out . . . . I instructed Private First Class Mobley, another guard, to get a flashlight and come with me. We then proceeded back to the tent. . . . We removed the drum from the hole. Mobley got down into the hole with the flashlight at which time he discovered a tunnel. I went back to the Control Office and informed Lieutenant Colonel Murdock and he, Major Williams, and Private First Class Terwilliger and myself went back . . . . As Terwilliger was smaller than any of us, I instructed him to go down into the tunnel and determine the extent of it. He took the flashlight and crawled through. Upon reaching the end of the tunnel he forced his nightstick up through the roof onto the surface, to indicate the tunnel's length. In the area of the tunnel we found various articles that had apparently been used to dig the tunnel. They included a shovel, boxes, cans and ropes. Also two flashlights were found in the area."

MP PRIVATE FIRST CLASS TERWILLIGER: "Sergeant First Class Logan directed me to . . . see if I could crawl into a tunnel which he had found . . . . I climbed down into a hole which was about four feet deep. I crawled into a tunnel which led off from the hole taking with me a flashlight and my nightstick. The tunnel began in one direction for about 2 feet and then angled off toward the stockade perimeter fences. It was just wide enough across for my shoulders and about one and one half feet high. Toward the end of the tunnel it became a little wider at which point I saw a small hole leading up to the surface. The hole was in the area between the two perimeter fences. The tunnel extended a bit further than the hole to a point directly below the concrete base of the outer perimeter fence. In the tunnel I found a broken shovel (Broken handle) and an empty coffee can, and a large metal rod."

On 13 September, investigators talked to and recorded the testimony of inmate Henry M. Wallace.

HENRY WALLACE: "Since the night of the riot . . . I slept in a large tent located in the Sentenced A area. There was another tent in the area located near the outer fence of which the men in that tent attempted to dig a tunnel. A prisoner named Harrison masterminded the digging of the tunnel. Other prisoners in the tent such as Soloman, Tilford, Mines, E., Victor, Ballard, Prather, Valquez and Rodriques along with Harrison and about two others helped with the digging. They used a shovel and butt cans for tools. The group mainly started the tunnel so that Tilford could escape but later, they planned to split into different groups and more would escape. The group also has a pair of pliers that they plan to use to cut the fence with if the tunnel fails. The plan was for them to escape during a certain time so that a certain guard would be on duty. They know the guard and knew that he wouldn't shoot them."

INVESTIGATOR: "Can you tell me when they plan to escape again?"

INMATE WALLACE: "I haven't heard but I know they are planning to try again."

INVESTIGATOR: "Where does the group keep the shovel and pliers that you mentioned?"

INMATE WALLACE: "The pliers is wire cutters and they keep the tools in the tent with them."

No escape efforts by tunneling ever succeeded. That was good fortune for the inmates who were involved. What could they have hoped to achieve? No matter how far they pushed a tunnel outside the wire, they would still have come to the surface inside the confines of Long Binh itself, a sprawling base the size of a small city. How could they have escaped notice on their way toward the perimeter of the base as they slunk through nighttime streets teeming with armed soldiers?

Even if they gained the open countryside and headed north, what could they have accomplished? Long Binh was more than six hundred miles from the Demilitarized Zone that divided the southern Republic of Viet Nam from the northern Democratic Republic of Viet Nam. Ha Noi was more than another four hundred miles to the north. They would have had to pass unnumbered U.S. Army and ARVN firebases and installations. They would have had to cross through heavily mined areas, through armed checkpoints. They would have had to slip around thousands of tiny Vietnamese hamlets unseen, to be certain that no villager saw them and reported their strange movement north. Whether black or white, non-Asians did not (and still do not) travel unnoticed across the face of Viet Nam.

What if they encountered Viet Cong or North Vietnamese units? No matter what they might hope to achieve once they reached Ha Noi, in the first moment of their sighting, such units would probably have brought them under fire. Unarmed, many would have died.

Nor would it have helped them if they chose to go west toward Cambodia rather than north. The distance would have been shorter, but the terrain was harsher. And even if they had reached sanctuary in Cambodia, they would still have no guarantee that they would be treated as anything other than enemy prisoners if they were captured rather than killed, a situation that would have shown them that life at LBJ might not have been so bad after all. Realistic appraisals were not, however, their strong point. All they knew was that they were miserable at LBJ and wanted out. If they could not do so by tunneling, perhaps there was another way.

Even as they continued their tunneling efforts, inmate leaders planned an alternate solution. At a predetermined time, prisoners would riot, taking control of LBJ. They would then throw open the gates and streams of men would flow out into the base of Long Binh. In the first confusing minutes they could seize weapons, trucks, armed jeeps and fight their way out of the encampment. What they would do then and where they would go was never clearly planned, but at least they would be free. Perhaps they could make it to Cambodia and across that troubled country into Thailand. Or perhaps they might still try to reach Ha Noi. They would worry about that later. First they had to take over the stockade. They could no longer tolerate the way they were being treated.

Perhaps not surprisingly, even the "worst" that former inmates recall about conditions in LBJ then does not sound much different from the way their brother soldiers in combat units lived. They complained about lock-downs, about being held in conex containers in DSEG. Would they rather have been on patrol in "Indian country," fearing that their next step forward might bring them into the killing zone of an ambush? Would they rather have been subjected to a mortar attack as they huddled in meager protection at a remote fire support base? They complained about the food. Would they rather have been quickly consuming C-rations during a hasty break on a search-and-destroy mission? *Everyone* in Viet Nam complained about the food. C-rations were noted for their caloric content, not their taste. Institutional food issuing from GI mess halls or kitchen tents prepared for those in rear areas soon begins to pall. Yet at LBJ prisoners and guards ate the same food prepared by the same personnel in the same mess hall. It was not inspired cookery, but it was always nutritious and sometimes even tasty.

Some prisoner complaints seemed to have been made solely for the sake of complaining. One inmate described his impression of conditions at LBJ. He was later shown to have been one of those who helped prepare for the riot.

INMATE PRIVATE GREGG PAYTON: "Let me tell you what the stockade was like, man. Maximum security had wooden bases with canvas roofs."

Was he criticizing the fact that at LBJ men could sleep under canvas and out of the mud, unlike many of those who served in combat units?

INMATE PAYTON: "They gave us dehydrated food—a big cauldron or pot of what was supposed to be Kool-Aid; one pack in fifteen gallons of water. Colored water. You dipped your cup in it and went to a slit-open sack of sugar and spooned sugar into it. You'd get a piece of meat that was so tough you could hardly chew it. Dehydrated potatoes. This was one of the things that created the climate for people who wanted to uprise, for the violence. If everything was peachy and creamy, who'd want to rock the apple boat? Tip over the apple cart? Conditions were really horrible, sanitation was ugly. A horrible kind of existence. And 90 percent were black African Americans."

Somehow this complaint is not compelling. A riot because of dehydrated potatoes? The problem had to have been more than Payton recalled. Another prisoner spoke of more concrete and substantial matters.

INMATE PRIVATE GERALD STOVALL: "What caused the riot? You gotta understand this was in 1968. King had been killed. When I was AWOL, guys in the Merchant Marine brought a lot of Black Panther literature over to us in Viet Nam. It was a consciousness-awakening thing for a lot of blacks. A lot of riots going on back in the States, and we knew of these riots from black troops coming In-Country. Even though there was a lot of camaraderie among black/white troops in combat, that wasn't true in the rear areas. A lot of blacks were perceiving the war as a white man's war."

A later confinement officer wondered about the causes of the riot.

MP LIEUTENANT COLONEL EUGENE MURDOCK: "I don't know what caused the initial flare-up there. I don't know whose fault it was, whether prisoner or guard. I imagine a combination thereof.

And the overcrowded condition. . . . I think inefficiency was what built the population up. The people [at correctional facilities] in Okinawa and other places didn't want them and so they didn't expedite shipments, and LBJ got more and more crowded before the riot. . . . 'Course they complained about the mess hall and food. I don't think that was the reason. It was just they were there, and hell, they were all just a bunch of hotheads. . . .

"The leaders were pretty damn sharp. They weren't fools. Not educated, but you don't have to be educated to be pretty damn clever. . . . Bunch of bastards."

A JAG officer who served as a courts-martial judge narrowed the focus of the problem. For him, the major cause of the riot was black/white hostility.

MAJOR JACK CROUCHET: "[P]eople in prison were either [already] convicted, in pretrial confinement, or awaiting discharge for administrative reasons. . . . The overcrowded conditions at the stockade contributed to the gradual tensions which had been building up for some time. . . . There is no question but that it was a racial incident . . . The prisoners were almost completely polarized into ethnic black and white groups. . . ."

George Deringer's deputy, Major Joshua Williams, himself an African American, believed that the flashpoint for the disturbance came because of Lieutenant Colonel Johnson's recent order to strip-search inmates entering LBJ in an effort to cut down on drug use. He spoke in the aftermath of the riot.

MAJOR WILLIAMS: "For the last few weeks there had been a lot of talk among the prisoners concerning the trouble they had at the Da Nang Stockade and the riot at a prison in Ohio. They indicated that the same thing would happen here. I would also say that the new search procedures initiated in the last few days, which reduced the introduction of contraband to include marijuana into the stockade, was a major contributing factor."

It was a well-organized group of inmates who planned and led the riot. The leader was probably Private Charles Planter. In the aftermath of the riot, one black inmate, himself one of those most active in the rioting, spoke about this small cluster of men. He testified to members of Detachment C, 8th Military Police Group (Criminal Investigation Detachment). In the transcript of that statement, he told of the way things were just prior to the riot.

INMATE PRIVATE FRANK TROUTMAN: "[T]here was a group that called theirselves the syndicate. Planter was head of the group . . . . This group had people shining shoes, doing their laundry, and everything else for them. . . . This group controlled the stockade as far as marijuana, any type pills, narcotics, and the stealing. This group used to talk practically daily that some day they would burn the place down."

Another inmate recalled Private Planter.

INMATE PAYTON: "I knew Planter. Planter was a guy from Connecticut. Very actionary kind of guy, very violent, wanted leadership. . . . Violent. Just like one of these Crips and Bloods. . . . He probably had some leadership talents. He had his band of merry men. . . . Maybe he wasn't natural; maybe it was forceful. Yeah, Planter was one of the organizers."

Who else numbered themselves as members of Planter's "merry men"? They included Private Jimi Childress, Private Harold Demetrius Beauchamps, Private David Coppege, Private James W. Anthony, Private Frank W. Troutman, Private Samuel Farmer, Private Ronald Cureton, Private Richard Cleveland—all blacks—and a Hispanic prisoner, Private Phillip E. Abano. During a later investigation, officials took testimony from Abano. A parenthetical note in the transcript of his testimony states: "Stockade officials identified Abano as one of six white men who participated with the hard core rioters." Presumably five other whites may also have been involved, but if so their names remain undiscovered.

Colonel Herbert Green affirmed that Private Charles Planter was the leader of the blacks in the stockade.

COLONEL GREEN: "However, he was not the leader of the riot. On the night of the riot Planter was being held [in DSEG] and was released only after much of the riot had occurred. . . . [Inmate Private David Coppege] was one of the leaders of the actual riot. Coppege had been tried and convicted twice before and was serving his sentence at the stockade. . . . On the night of the riot Coppege led a gang . . . into the Administration Compound. He was the first person at the gates. He . . . was pushing and pulling at the gate and when a sergeant tried to quell the rioters at the gate, Coppege was the first person to punch that sergeant."

INMATE STOVALL: "Another guy we called 'Wild Bill' Childress. He was one of the architects of the riot. . . . [K]nowin' Wild Bill, I know he was one of the ones who was a architect . . . . He was very militant minded. . . . Very vocal. He started going around tellin' guys we got to start makin' changes, got to stop people from doin' stuff."

As plans developed, certain trusted inmates were assigned various tasks to help the scheme along.

INMATE PAYTON: "What I did [prior to the riot] was to bring in the kerosene for the fires. My job in minimum security was to burn feces and I would go out every day in the truck to . . . the hospital and different places . . . . Certain people asked me . . . if I could bring in extra kerosene. . . . [T]hey said we're going to do this. . . . [W]hen the organizer came to me it was like well yeah, okay, man. I was saying to myself this guy's full of shit. They had little caucus meetings and I sat in on a couple of them. Clandestine. Lights out. People sneaking around the barracks. . . . So every other day I would bring in extra cans . . . . We kept it right there in front of the guards. . . . I built up some extra cans. They didn't know which cans were empty and which cans were full. . . . [A] lot of the guards weren't really MP-trained. One guy smuggled a watermelon through two or three checkpoints. Where there's a will there's a way."

As D-Day grew closer, activity intensified. Syndicate leaders knew that the initial frenzy at the moment the riot began could be heightened if some were high on drugs. One of the riot leaders testified that in the hours prior to the riot, one guard supplied them with marijuana.

INMATE PRIVATE DAVID COPPEGE: "[Another man, a tower guard] dropped five pill boxes inside the compound [that] contained Binoctal tablets."

Other inmates confirmed such testimony.

INMATE PRIVATE DAVID L. ZELLER: "I was visiting a friend . . . in the medium compound on the day before the riot. It was approximately 1300 hours [1 P.M.], 28 August 1968, when I observed several Negroes that sleep in the same tent leave and go out by the fence near the guard tower. I saw the tower guard throw two packages of cigarettes, one syringe and needle and a package of Binoctal tablets over to the Negroes standing by the fence."

———————

Then it all began. There were, on 29 August 1968, 719 inmates held at LBJ, a facility built to house half that number. The daylight faded. Guards patrolling the compound neither saw nor sensed any more tension than "normal." The early night hours seemed to pose no new problems.

INMATE PRIVATE JEREMIAH JAMES: "The riot had been planned, but it went off earlier than scheduled due to the increased beating."

It is impossible to tell what beatings James referred to. No evidence suggests that guards had been any rougher during the days preceding the riot. Whatever the reason, members of the syndicate gave the signal. Those locked in cells began to free themselves. Berry writes, "With almost admirable ingenuity, the filters of cigarettes had been stuffed into the locks on cells and set afire; of course that [later] led to the rule against filter cigarettes in the stockade."[1] Presumably the heat softened the metal of the locks, and the cell doors were forced open.

INMATE PRIVATE GREGG PAYTON: "The synchronization of the riot was great. I was asleep and half high when it went off."

The rioting began at approximately 11:45 P.M. Most of the prisoners were caught by surprise at the sudden activity, the shouts, the sounds of running feet. Nevertheless, they reacted swiftly. But even after the disturbance guards did not at first sound any alarms or take any unusual precautionary measures.

———————

[1]Berry, *Those Gallant Men,* p. 84.

At the same time as some inmates were trying to get out of their conex cells, over in the detainee section of B Compound (Medium) a small group of presentenced prisoners forcibly removed the compound gate key from an on-duty guard. Simultaneously, sentenced inmates in B Section of B Compound overpowered a gate guard who was in the process of opening the gate for another guard.

One guard, whose name was removed from the official report on the riot, said that from what he saw, the whole thing started in B Compound of medium security.

By 11:50 P.M. those from the two sections began to pour into the exercise area. Strangely enough, despite all the recent talk by members of the syndicate, that night they made no concerted effort to escape. Inmate rage—a later report called it "planned and unbridled violence by blacks against Caucasians"—seemed to fuel the activity rather than any desire to get outside the confines of LBJ.

Rioters tried to arm themselves as best they could. Some carried torches made of rolled newspapers soaked in gasoline. Others carried bunk adapters, metal or wood bars torn from bunks. Prisoners wrenched boards from buildings to use as clubs. As the turmoil grew, inmates invaded the mess hall and snatched up cooking knives.

Guards in the Sentenced A Compound area heard noises and went outside and secured the gate from that compound that led to the exercise area side. Other MPs managed to sound a general alarm. The news that something unusual was happening within the wire began to spread. A computation clerk at the compound told how he was affected.

MIKE DOHERTY: "We were called to fall out for the stockade about eleven or twelve [o'clock] that night. We had not had riot control training. We saw guards inside running for their lives out through the main gate. Some guards climbed the fence and through the roll of concertina wire at the top to . . . save their lives."

The securing of the A Section gate did not help for long. It took only five minutes for inmates in the Sentenced A area to scale and break through the fence to join those already gathered and milling about in the exercise area of B Compound (medium). The savage beatings of guards and other prisoners began.

GUARD LOUIS J. ZARRELLI: "I was kicked and punched . . . . The two ring leaders who were trying to break open the Maximum gate were Prisoner Coppege and Prisoner Beauchamps. They were the two who stood out . . . . They were yelling at the prisoners inside to 'kill those white mother-fucking guards.' I made it a point to remember those two."

By midnight inmates were moving through the control gate toward the stockade's administrative office and the DSEG area. As they advanced, they overpowered guards and set free selected prisoners. Inmates in A Compound (minimum) forced their gate from the inside and they, along with others from B Compound, now moved into the center of the stockade where the administration buildings were located.

⸻

Wrathful violence of the rioting black prisoners flowed two ways: toward any available guard whether black or white and toward any handy white inmate. For a time some blacks tried to protect whites.

INMATE PRIVATE GERALD STOVALL: "So when the riot hopped off, you had guys, some combat soldiers, who still tried to keep up camaraderie and at the same time you had blacks from rear areas caught up in the belief that it was us against them. . . . I remember this one guy tied up this white guy and started beatin' him with a two-by-four, and some blacks ran over to him and said, 'Hey man, don't *do* that. It's not about that!' For some it was a black/white, get-anything-you-can thing. For others it was us against them. Prisoners against those in power. It went both ways."

Such efforts to protect white inmates, however, soon came to an end.

One unnamed white inmate told how Ronald Cureton, a black inmate, ran up to Phillip MaGee, a white prisoner, and hit him several times in the head with a bunk adapter. "[B]lack prisoners were tying the hands of the white prisoners behind their backs and using the white prisoners as shields against the guards."

INMATE COPPEGE: "[I saw Captain Jones trying to] talk to a bunch of the Negroes. . . . The Negroes wouldn't listen to him and they started swinging at him. Captain Jones ran [but] Reese stuck his foot out and tripped [him]. At this time Caffey started kicking and hitting Captain Jones and Ronald Hiath hit [him] with a baseball bat. Several other people jumped on [him]."

WHITE INMATE PRIVATE DONALD N. ALBERTSON: "[A]bout midnight I awoke to hear a lot of yelling. . . . About 15 or 20 of us white prisoners took refuge in parollee tent #1."

WHITE INMATE PRIVATE DONALD E. TABLER: "I was awaken by hearing someone yelling 'please have Mercy'. . . . I [saw] two colored guys . . . beating a tall blond headed, husky build fellow with broken boards. It appeared that they jabbed him with the broken ends. . . . They really messed his face up. [A black minimum prisoner] backed me up against the wall with a razor blade against my neck and told me 'If you talk, I will cut your chuck throat.'"

BLACK INMATE PRIVATE JAMES M. ANTHONY: "I picked [up] a stick [and] while I was standing there a white man came up to me and said something . . . [When he did] I hit him across the shoulders right behind the neck with the stick. The man did not fall. At this time Jessie Green had a round metal object that was about 3–4 feet long in his hand. Green hit the man around the forehead or temple part of the head with the metal object he had. The man fell to the ground and at this time Green hit the man on the head again . . . ."

WHITE INMATE PRIVATE RONALD J. BASS: "We went outside and was assaulted by several Negros who beat and kicked us. A man I know by the name of CanTu [Ronald Cureton] beat me and held a razor blade at my throat."

WHITE INMATE PRIVATE JOSEPH F. BULLARD: "The Negro prisoners refer to white prisoners as 'chucks'. . . . The yard was full of Negroes who were yelling 'Kill the chucks.'"

WHITE INMATE PRIVATE ANTONIO B. CATENACCI: "Some were trying to set tents on fire and others were kicking over water barrels."

John T. Fanning was a white MP inprocessing clerk who worked in the administration building: "I made a mad dash for the front gate of the Medium Compound. I knew then for sure that it was a racial thing; I could hear all the yelling, 'Get the chucks!' The gate was just opening when I got to it. Both Negro and white prisoners were like a human wave—everyone trying to get out. I made it to the Control Room. . . . Some Negro prisoners came in carrying baseball bats. . . . When I first got to the Stockade in June, the Negroes weren't as militant and aggressive . . . . It's steadily been getting worse as living conditions have been getting better. . . . In June there were only 6–10 troublemakers; now there are 80–100."

In testimony later given to the CID detachment as its members investigated what happened that night, syndicate leaders, desperate to shift blame from themselves, reported on fellow members of their group. With their words they incriminated those who only a few days before had been their "bro." One such was Samuel Lester Farmer who, despite his testimony, was court-martialed.

INMATE PRIVATE SAMUEL FARMER: "[T]here were a few individuals who stood out among the crowd. . . . [One was] Soloman, I. He was running around with a bunk adapter yelling 'let's kill these chucks' and he also helped to burn down the mess hall and also helped to break into the box. Childress, he helped start the fires, he burned the following places: mess hall, admin building and the finance building . . . ."

An MP captain who was duty officer that night, ALPHONSO A. FROST: "It was confusion in trying to quell the prisoners and fight the fires."

One guard on duty that night had gone to the mess hall for midnight chow prior to the outbreak. He returned to work about 11:45 P.M.

GUARD J. P. MOBLEY: "I saw five or six prisoners ganged up around one of the other guards, named Rockholdt. . . . . They suddenly started beating Rockholdt and had knocked him to the ground. I started blowing my whistle and ran to the gate. Two of the prisoners grabbed me and had me in a position with my arms locked to my side."

He fought them and they ran, taking his helmet liner with them.

WHITE INMATE PRIVATE CHARLES H. MONTGOMERY: "There was smoke in the area and I looked over towards the medium compound and it looked like the whole place was ablaze. . . . [T]here was about 50 to 75 men around the fence. I knew it was a race riot, because they were all Negroes and they were all yelling 'Let's get those chucks'. . . . [T]he Negroes started coming in at us. They were swinging bunk adapters and boards. Some of them had butcher knives. . . . [A] Negroid male hit a white man in the face [with a bunk adapter] and it almost took off his nose. . . . They started pushing us and made us line out along the fence. . . . [They asked one guy] what is my color and the guy said brown and the Negroid said no, beautiful black and told the guy to say this. The man said it. Then they started with the clubs again and they kept saying 'We're going to kill all you chucks.'"

Montgomery ran away and got to the guards who put him in protective custody.

MP SPECIALIST FOURTH CLASS GUARD DENNIS W. RYAN: "Troutman had a blond, rectangular piece of wood, about two and a half feet in length and was beating on a white prisoner with it. I saw and heard him strike this man about seven or eight times, on the head with this stick."

WHITE INMATE PRIVATE MARK P. SCHERTZER: "A colored male who I know as 'Tom,' . . . came running into the compound carrying a large stick and yelling 'Let's kill all of them chucks.' Tom then walked up beside Tent #17, leaned over inside . . . and struck a sleeping white male twice on the head . . . ."

WHITE INMATE PRIVATE DENNIS M. SULLIVAN: "[A]nother Negro . . . was pacing up and down in front of our tent yelling 'You stupid fucking fools, you're doing it all wrong.'"

WHITE INMATE PRIVATE LEONARD L. THURMES: "I stood there and watched with the other caucasian males . . . . [W]e saw the Negroes coming toward us with sticks, razors, boards and bunk adaptors . . . we began trying to climb over the fence . . . so that no one could come after us. As we climbed to the top of the fence, we were told by the tower guard to get down off of the fence or that he would shoot."

An unnamed white inmate commented: "One of the Negroes had a razor type weapon in his hand and he assaulted me with it. I put out my hand to protect my face and the razor type weapon cut my hand. . . . [T]he remainder of the group started hitting me with sticks. . . . mostly on the back . . . . I fell to the floor and pretended I was unconscious."

Another man, whose name was not given in the official report, said: "[T]he Negroes then made some of the whites take off their boots and give them to the Negroes who in turn removed the shoe-strings and utilized them to tie the hands of the whites behind their backs. . . . and began to beat them with sticks and bunk adapters. . . . [T]hree Negroes . . . came up and stated that 'How does it feel now for you to be the minority'. . . . I was also assaulted by a Negro male who held a razor blade at my throat. . . . [G]uards was approaching the gate and he used me as a hostage to keep them from entering."

A white inmate told how "[This one black said that] all of the chucks were going to die in about two minutes. . . . Some MPs were moving in our direction . . . and a [black] man . . . went over to two caucasians . . . and made them lie on the ground face down and he said, 'if any of those guards stab a brother with their bayonets, these chucks are going to die.'"

A white inmate testified, "I was awakened (about 1 A.M.) and someone was screaming that Charlie was in the compound and that he was coming to 'break the brothers out.' [Name deleted] had a bunk adapter in his hand and was screaming to the guards that if a colored inmate died then 5 white guys would die."

Another white inmate remembered that "The Negroes began attacking us with bunk adapters, knives, steel bars from beds, boots, and just about anything they could get their hands on. . . . One of the[ir] group was a caucasian parolee. . . .[H]e was with them when they forced us against the fence. I heard him make the comment that he was going to show his brothers how to 'fuck a chuck up good' or words to that effect. He . . . kicked me in the chest. I was kicked in the testicles and stomach by two Negroes. . . . The Caucasian who was kicking prisoners is a parolee with a tattoo of a bull over his left breast and the name Ken on his right arm."

COLONEL HERBERT GREEN: "Throughout the riot beatings occurred in various parts of the compound. In fact one [white] pris-oner was beaten to death in the minimum compound."

That man was Private Edward Haskett of St. Petersburg, Florida, beaten to death with a shovel, his skull crushed.

COLONEL HERBERT GREEN: "[P]risoners gathered blankets and mattresses and set them on fire. Tents were burned, office equipment broken and all sorts of property destroyed."

Inmate David Coppege, who testified so easily against fellow members of the syndicate after the riot failed, was himself very noticeable during the violence.

COLONEL GREEN: "Subsequently, Coppege went into the mess hall and then went to the area euphemistically called the Adjustment Center [DSEG]. This area, surrounded by a fence, was composed of single cells. . . . and was known as The Box. Coppege led the group . . . who gained access to this area. He went through . . . unlocking cells and releasing black prisoners. He did not release any white prisoners. . . . He was the . . . main protagonist in The Box area. . . . Coppege then secured a liquid he thought to be gasoline and began pouring it throughout the area. He then obtained matches and struck some in an attempt to ignite the liquid. Fortunately, a fire, which would have killed several individuals did not occur. After his unsuccessful arson attempt, Coppege went outside The Box and what occurred next was one of the true miracles of the event.

"Two of the guards, both white, had climbed on top of The Box to get away from the rioters [who] were . . . predominantly, if not all, black. They were yelling 'Kill the guards,' 'Kill the chucks' and other similar phrases.

"Coppege not only joined in the clamor but was probably leading it. The two guards believed they were about to be killed or at the very least severely injured. At that point [inmate] Private Charles Planter approached the guards and told them that if they came down, he would escort them out of the stockade and that they would not be injured. The guards climb[ed] down off the roof of The Box and followed Planter across the entire Administration Compound and out the main gate. Although rioters were everywhere, no one touched the guards and they escaped unscathed."

Inmate Coppege was court-martialed the following December for his part in the riots. He was found guilty, given a dishonorable discharge, and sentenced to fifteen years confinement. Private Planter was never tried for anything that occurred that night of the riot because officials determined that he was not a major participant. He was also given credit for having saved the lives of several guards. As a postscript, Planter's conviction that had originally placed him in the stockade was subsequently overturned on appeal in 1969.

The night was not yet over. Flames cast their yellow glare across the burning compound. Men bent on violence still roamed the stockade. Outside the gates a military reaction force gathered from all over the Long Binh area, but those inside were determined not to surrender in the face of that superior strength. They were still intent on violence.

# CHAPTER EIGHT

# FACED BY
# SUPERIOR FORCE

Only a few minutes after the riot began confinement officer Lieutenant Colonel Vernon D. Johnson received word of the violence breaking out within the LBJ compound. He was probably asleep in his quarters when someone pounded on his door. What he felt as he first heard the news is not known. All efforts to interview him were refused. Did he have an element of concern for his career? A riot at LBJ while he was in command would not look good on his record at promotion time. Frustration? He had been there only a short time, not enough to resolve all the issues that boiled beneath the surface. Anger? Why would his inmates do such a thing when he had tried hard to make their lives a little better? He had listened to them when they had complaints and even sometimes had ruled on their behalf against the wishes of custodial staff.

A few minutes before midnight, he arrived at the gates of the stockade. His responsibility was to stop this insurrection before the whole facility fell into chaos. There was already enough obvious turmoil as it was. Fires were burning. Men were rampaging. Some fled for their lives. He could hear angry shouts and curses. Perhaps he stood at the gate for a moment while he considered options. Then he decided. He would go into the midst of these prisoners and talk some sense into their heads.

MP FIRST LIEUTENANT ERNEST B. TALPS: "Lieutenant

Colonel Johnson came into the stockade at the gate and I met him at his office."

The two men talked, Talps giving Johnson what little information he had about what was happening. The 89th MP Group and other units from all over the Long Binh installation had already begun to respond to the threat. Tower guards had been reinforced. Hastily convened MPs were guarding the perimeter wire to prevent escapes. By ten minutes after midnight fire trucks began arriving. So also did the first ambulance, and willing hands began evacuating injured men to the 24th Medical Evacuation Hospital. Within ten more minutes the first reaction-force troops were positioned around the stockade, wearing steel pots and protective vests and carrying rifles and tear gas grenades. They stood awaiting orders.

A few minutes after midnight, Lieutenant Colonel Johnson, accompanied by Talps, walked unarmed into the compound toward the rioting prisoners. They strode directly toward the mess hall.

They were not, however, the first officers who had confronted the rioters. That man was a Captain Jones.

WHITE INMATE PRIVATE JOSEPH F. BULLARD: "Captain Frost came running to the small gate yelling that Captain Jones was being beaten up."

FIRST LIEUTENANT ERNEST B. TALPS: "I found Captain Jones lying on the ground by the control building . . . ."

CLERK MIKE DOHERTY: "When the riot started [Johnson] thought he could stop it and took a young captain with him to quell the action. They went into the stockade without weapons. Prisoners jumped them both, and they were beaten up badly."

INMATE PRIVATE JOSEPH F. BULLARD: "A little while later, I saw Lieutenant Colonel Johnson come through the small gate and go run into the mob that was in the middle of the compound. In a couple of minutes he came back . . . with his face all beaten and bloody."

BLACK INMATE PRIVATE GERALD STOVALL: "I saw the colonel when he got all beat up. [laughs] Yeah. I saw that. Well, what happened was, he stood there tryin' to talk to everybody: blip, blip, blip, blip. Some guys had gone into the mess hall and got food . . .

and stood there while the colonel was talkin'. He was very adamant with his hands, wavin' them, and he knocked the food out of one guy's hands and the guy took that very personal. They went to work on him, man. It surprised me that he lived through it."

18TH MILITARY POLICE BRIGADE STAFF SECTION OFFICER O. LYNN MCCOTTER: "[Harold Demetrius] Beauchamps was the guy they think attacked Colonel Johnson."

FIRST LIEUTENANT TALPS: "He became involved in an argument with a prisoner, C. Planter [just released from his conex box cell by other inmates], who was screaming at the colonel 'I told you it was going to happen. I told you they were going to do it.'"

Johnson told Talps to take Planter out of the compound. He started back toward the gate with Planter in tow. Memories of what he saw next would long remain vivid.

FIRST LIEUTENANT TALPS: "I saw Lieutenant Colonel Johnson running towards the main gate . . . near the personal property building. I . . . saw that he was staggering and almost stumbling. He was bleeding about the head. I helped him out the gate and had some MPs rush him to the hospital."

BLACK INMATE PRIVATE FRANK TROUTMAN: "Lieutenant Colonel Johnson was trying to talk and someone said, 'Fire that Chuck up.' Someone . . . hit [him] with a fist and then people started hitting him with fists and bunk adapters."

Another inmate identified as having struck Johnson was Henry Wallace.

BLACK INMATE PRIVATE DAVID COPPEGE: "Several of the Negroes spotted the Colonel at the corner of the mess hall and a bunch of them jumped on him. After the Colonel was beat up he finally got up and ran out the gate."

DEPUTY PROVOST MARSHAL LIEUTENANT COLONEL CLAUDE K. FOUAD: "A group of eight formed a cordon and got Johnson out. He was taken to the hospital. For the next few days we kept up with Johnson's condition and he was in a pretty bad state. Then he was evacuated back to CONUS."

Colonel Johnson was not the only high-ranking officer to try to stem the violence. His deputy, Major Joshua Williams, a black man, also did his best. He went inside the compound, walked to the chapel steps, and tried to talk to some of the rioters.

INMATE TROUTMAN: "Some were yelling to fire the Tom up and others were yelling to let him speak."

INMATE COPPEGE: "At this time Major Williams had got on the Chapel steps and was trying to talk to the Negroes. They wouldn't listen to him and I tried to get them to listen . . . . I told them I had known [him] back on the block and he was OK. They listened for two to maybe four minutes but it didn't do any good. . . . When they wouldn't listen, the Major left."

Elsewhere throughout the stockade the violence continued.

INMATE TROUTMAN: "Some of the white guys were being pulled from the fence and beaten by the Negroes with fists and bunk adapters. Jody Smith was walking back and forth in front of the white guys telling them how much he hated them and asking how it felt to be on the bottom. . . . I grabbed [a white man] by the collar and drug him over to the guards and said look how half your people look already. Do you want all your guys to look like this[?]"

INMATE STOVALL: "There was another guy, a guard, layin' right in front of the control tower where everybody who ran past him hit him in the head with a bunk adapter. His head started soundin' like a piece of watermelon. No movement. Nothin, you know? These guys were mad, man, I tell you. . . . That white guard who was laid out in front of the control tower the night of the riot and who got hit in the head by the bunk adapters—I don't remember his name but I remember him being *very* nasty. He was one of those guys the others couldn't wait until they had an opportunity to get to him and when they did they really let him have it."

Flames burnt brightly everywhere, illuminating the stockade. Former tents were piles of ashes. The mess hall was torched, still burning to the ground. The supply building slowly collapsed upon itself. The interior of the administration building lay gutted from fire. Knots of armed and angry inmates roamed the compound, looking for more victims. In all the confusion of that night, some prisoners may have escaped, at least according to the claim of one prisoner.

BLACK INMATE PRIVATE GREGG PAYTON: "On the night of the riot the records room was burned down and there was a guy trapped in there and we pulled away the boards on the side of the building to help him get out. Some guys escaped. They beat up some MPs and took their uniforms, dressed up, and walked out. I saw them later in Saigon. They were downtown still masquerading as MPs."

Not all black inmates sought out whites to attack as revenge for their plight. Even some of those who had helped prepare for the riot refrained from participating.

INMATE STOVALL: "The night it hopped off I made a beeline straight for the supply room to get me a gas mask 'cause I knew the gas was comin'. That was one of the reasons we were able to hold them off so long because most of us had gas masks but eventually we had to give up because a lot of guys didn't have them. That kind of hurt us."

Other men, most of the whites and many black inmates, simply wanted nothing to do with the riot. They sought only safety from the rampaging mob. Within thirty minutes of the start of the new day, guards began supervising the removal of prisoners not participating in the disorder from the LBJ compound.

MP DEPUTY PROVOST MARSHAL CLAUDE K. FOUAD: "There were a lot of the prisoners who wanted to get out and didn't want to have any part of what was going on. So we were able to go in and get those prisoners out. We took them outside of the stockade and put them in the middle of a field where we could keep them as a group. In order to see we got military vehicles with headlights on and ringed the area where the prisoners were in the center. . . . Inside they were still tearing everything up."

FIRST LIEUTENANT TALPS: "I was picking up bodies of prisoners left and right. I got two in the medium compartment prisoners fall-out area. They were both Caucasian . . . . At this time the mess hall, in-processing, personal property and maybe the supply building were all on fire."

MP COMPUTATION CLERK MIKE DOHERTY: "The prisoners controlled the stockade the night of the riot. [They] burnt everything to the ground . . . they destroyed files. . . . We had an administrative nightmare for awhile, figuring out what the prisoners' sentences had been . . . . We sent notices to their companies asking them to forward to us copies of their court-martial records. They [also] went into the infirmary and confiscated drugs and got high."

In later years, men offered wild memories of how the reaction-force troops had assembled at the stockade, then entered LBJ to stop the rioters and ended the insurrection. These recollections came both from prisoners and from MPs, proving that even eyewitness testimony can often be very wrong.

BLACK INMATE PRIVATE JEREMIAH JAMES: "Eighteen dead—two by the security force, the others killed by other prisoners. Two of the most brutal killings . . . were when the security force came in. They weren't organized and before they got comfortable, prisoners snatched them out of formation, handcuffed them to the fence and beat them to death."

INMATE STOVALL: "The medium section was burned down forcing everyone into the minimum section. Everybody is hollerin' and throwin' things at the MPs and they start shootin'. So some black brothers said, 'Let's put some white guys up in front of us. Everybody knows they're not going to shoot them.' Well the MPs stopped that in a minute. They shot at everybody!"

MP DEPUTY PROVOST MARSHAL CLAUDE K. FOUAD: "Our instructions were not to fire. The only time you fire is if you are in peril of losing your life. I do not recall any gunfire. We went in unarmed. You were not going to give a prisoner an opportunity to get your weapon. That's SOP [standing operating procedure]."

MP PRIVATE FIRST CLASS THOMAS MCKEON: "When I arrived In-Country, I was assigned to the 90th Replacement Company at Bien Hoa. [After] three days a three-quarter-ton truck picked me up and took me to the 720th MP BN [at LBJ]. 'You're going to LBJ.' [It was] the third day of the rioting. . . . Our barracks was one street over from the jail. We were the only combat MPs in Viet Nam. . . . the reaction force for the post and the stockade. We were the ones who went in and put it down. . . . We heard all kinds of stories [about what had happened].

"[We heard about] blacks . . . [who'd] come by in a deuce and a half or ten ton truck . . . and stand on top. They'd be really close to the top of the fence . . . and they would heave weapons over the fence into the exercise yard. The rioters didn't use them because they were afraid to. Open gun jeeps with M-50s [machine guns] were lined up on them. M-113 APCs [armored personnel carriers] too."

DEPUTY PROVOST MARSHAL FOUAD: "No weapons were thrown over the fence to my knowledge. I was one of the people responsible for getting the thing under control. We had traffic control points blocking the roads. All traffic was blocked by emergency vehicles."

MP PRIVATE FIRST CLASS MCKEON: "They had us wearing flak jackets, MP brassards, steel pots, gas masks, each man was issued two gas grenades, M-14 rifles with unsheathed fixed bayonets and a full load of ammo locked and loaded. My squad leader asked me if I had any problems with using the bayonet. No, I said. . . . Then we went in . . . in double rows in V formation, with the foot stomp, NCOs right behind us. When you stomp you're lunging at the same time . . . it was just getting dark. . . . The [rioters] had strands of barbed wire, maybe six, cut in two foot lengths with duct tape for a grip and they were swinging those at us, plus they were throwing debris over the heads of people in front of them. . . . We bayonetted a lot of them. We *stuck* them; we impaled them with the bayonet. In the body. I know of three who died against the fence. Their entrails were hanging out. I saw this. . . . When we got done, there were about seven of them laying at the base of our formation. Two of them I know had to die, because they were gutted. . . . When I got back it was dark, about 9 or 10 o'clock. We never had to go in again."

McKeon's time line is incorrect. The riot began just before midnight on 29 August, and by 2 A.M. the following day, 30 August, the situation was at least partly under control. Yet he speaks of going in when "it was just getting dark" and after going into the prison in riot formation and subduing the prisoners, it was only "about 9 or 10 o'clock" in the evening. At that time, the riot had not yet even begun.

By 5:30 A.M. on 30 August, most of those who wanted to get out of the stockade had done so, and the security force had rounded up many of the militant prisoners. The latter were put under confinement in an open field on the north side of the stockade. Inside the wire, however, a great many men remained who had not surrendered and, for a time, they were left alone on orders from high authority.

Shortly after the start of the riot, news of what was happening reached high commanders—18th Military Police Brigade, 89th Military Police Group, and those at the United States Army, Vietnam (USARV) at Long Binh. General Frank T. Mildren was commander of USARV.

GENERAL MILDREN: "[N]one of the prisoners had gotten out because the outer inclosures still held. Those who had created the disturbance were over in the maximum security area . . . . I found that the number of rioters was probably 100 . . . . [out of a population of] between 700 and 800 . . . . [T]he total number of prisoners was almost double what it should have been.

". . . I refused to storm the stockade and said that we were just going to bide our time until daylight and then take a good look . . . . CBS descended. [N]ewspaper reporters descended . . . . CBS demanded that they be allowed to go inside . . . and interview these people with TV and microphones. I said 'Not on your bottom dollar . . . . you will get one picture and the wrong one from those characters.'"[1]

In the early morning hours of 30 August, General Mildren reached out to contact two field grade MP officers on assignment elsewhere in Viet Nam. With Colonel Johnson injured and hospitalized, someone needed to step in as acting confinement officer, and to do so immediately. General Mildren gave orders that Lieutenant Colonel Eugene "Big Gene" Murdock and Lieutenant Colonel Herman Trop, both MP officers, were to report to Long Binh as soon as possible. They reported to the general before the day ended.

Both in the same small branch of the Army, Murdock and Trop had known each other for some years. Now, for the next few weeks, they would work together to put the stockade back into proper order.

---

[1]Mildren's comments are taken from the Frank T. Mildren Oral History, U.S. Army Military History Institute, Carlisle Barracks, Pa.

Murdock was in charge, Trop his deputy. Colonel Trop believed he had given General Mildren, in an early meeting soon after his arrival, the proper course of action to follow.

LIEUTENANT COLONEL TROP: "General Milburn [*sic*] and some staff members . . . . were talking about going in there with riot control . . . with force and/or starving them out. I took over the conversation and told General Milburn that this would not work."

This is hindsight at its best. A lieutenant colonel does not "take over" a staff meeting presided over by a full general. Nor does a lieutenant colonel "tell" a general *anything*; certainly he does not tell a general that he is wrong. He might make carefully considered "suggestions," but the decisions are always made by the ranking officer present.

LIEUTENANT COLONEL TROP: "There were two hundred-some [rioting inmates]. . . . If we acted like gentlemen—treated them fairly as officers should treat EM [enlisted men]—we were going to deal with some of them. . . . My suggestion was to feed them. His staff then said 'Let's take the cigarettes out of the C-rations.' I suggested not to do so. Take the coffee out. I said No. Just give them the rations as they were. Let's don't screw around. We have to look better than they do. We would break it quicker by not nitpicking."

Colonel Murdock recalled that it was he who spoke with Mildren.

EUGENE MURDOCK: "[General] Frank Mildren said to me: 'Can you go in there and take them?' I said, 'Yessir'. . . . It was eerie walking through the gate and the damn ole lights and smoke, buildings still burning, wire all around and that bunch over there going BOUGA-LOU, BOUGALOU, BOUGALOU. . . . Minimum number of escapes. . . . maybe only three or four who left the compound; maybe as many as seven. They came back, all but a couple and I think they ended up dead down in Dope Alley in Saigon, down there with the whores, drug addicts. Soul Alley.

"We could have gone in there anytime we wanted. . . . All kind of things we could have done. . . . We'd of wiped their ass. We left them alone. [Any chance of escape] was over in two-three hours. . . . There wasn't much accomplished the first few days other than to keep it *down* and keep things moving and no big moves. . . . Inmates had one compound they was in command of. They were all black. . . . Percentage was way up there. It *had* to be 80–85 percent. . . . Let them stay there. They're not going anywhere."

GENERAL MILDREN: "[A]fter one day . . . these people had turbans on their heads and homemade robes, and it looked like somebody out of Africa in there."

INMATE PRIVATE GERALD STOVALL: "After the first night of the riot we slept in Big Red. Half the compound had burned down and there was nowhere else for us. They [the authorities] brought blankets and tents in for us. We used them for other things. We used the blankets to make African robes and the tent poles for spears, because that is where our head was at the time."

INMATE PRIVATE JEREMIAH JAMES: "Guys went back completely to African customs and dress. They used sheets and tore headbands to wear and took off their clothes and made African clothes out of sheets. They took some other sheets, wet them, and stretched them over barrels and drummed on them. It was just nuts."

MP LIEUTENANT COLONEL MURDOCK: "Those blacks turned native. They wore blankets and put chicken bones in their hair and tied them in their nose. Beat on barrels for drums. . . . No, I don't understand [people] who put goddam chicken bones in their nose and their hair. . . . If a supply room doesn't issue you a chicken bone, you don't get it."

CLERK DOHERTY: "They beat on drums like tom-toms for awhile. We just backed off. We threw bread over the fences so they had something to eat and put water inside the gate and just waited them out. As they'd give up and come out we put them in temporary stockade a little distance away."

GENERAL MILDREN: "[D]ays went on . . . . My staff was getting itchy. . . . after three or four days . . . a few of these prisoners wanted out so we opened the gates and brought them out . . . and put them over in another enclosure. That went on for over a week . . . until we got down to the hard core . . . of 13 . . . the people who had organized and done this.

"I said, . . . We'll toss some C-rations over to them periodically . . .

but be sure you take all the cigarettes . . . and all the candy and other goodies out . . . just give them the basics."

LIEUTENANT COLONEL TROP: "We piled C-ration cases up at the gate after they came off the truck. We took the wires and sleeves off the cartons and opened the gate and let the prisoners' representatives come get them. Within ten minutes there was the biggest fooforaw you ever did hear. Fighting and hollering. Cursing. One of the ringleaders, wearing a breech cloth and leather vest and his head shaved—absolutely wild—from someplace in New York, came out and was abusing everyone there that we had shorted the rations. I told him very calmly to come out and count the C-ration cartons sleeves. He wouldn't come out at first because he was afraid we would lock him up, but he finally did. Twelve more rations went in than there were prisoners. I said to him: 'What it is, your own people are in there doing this to each other.' He went back and there was a fight, and there was a fire later in the evening that caused no damage that I know of.

"The next morning I was standing out by the gate about 5:30 or 6:00, drinking a canteen cup of coffee and smoking a cigar, and two black prisoners walked up to the gate and, after a bit of conversation, asked how they could get out of there. And that was the break. Within a couple of days it was about over. I feel mine was a commonsense approach to a very touchy situation."

So Colonel Trop believed his were the efforts that resolved the aftereffects of the riot at LBJ. Perhaps not surprisingly, General Mildren believed that his own wise leadership ended the disturbance. And "Big Gene" Murdock believed he, as the ranking officer at LBJ, might have had something to do with the riot's resolution. In their accounts, Mildren and Trop told only of what they had done, each taking credit for restoring order to the stockade. In his interview, Murdock was charitable enough to recall what others had done and to credit Trop for his efforts to lighten an otherwise deadly serious situation although he took forceful action as well. He recalled how the inmates, in the days after the riot, continued to bang on their homemade drums.

LIEUTENANT COLONEL MURDOCK: "Ole Trop went out there one night and said, 'Alright, this is the last time I'm going to tell you—I want you to tune that sonofabitch up!'

"Trop was great. . . . He'd go out there and they'd start hollering and he'd throw a couple of gas grenades over the fence into them. Scatter them for a little bit . . . . [W]e'd get these calls every damn night from Washington. . . . Trop said, 'They can kiss my ass.' He'd be sitting there typing up a report and they'd call and he'd say, 'Now gentlemen, what can I do for you?' and he'd reach down and grab his balls. We'd all laugh.

"The first week [inmates would try to run up the high outer fence in an effort to escape]. So Ole Trop went out and got a bunch of bamboo poles. They'd run out to the fence and start climbing and he'd take one of those poles and *whap* the shit out of them, about break their damn knuckles. Down they'd come! Then he'd hand them a tear gas baseball grenade. They made us stop that cause the hospital was just right up from us and it had air conditioning and they were inhaling all that tear gas.

"Every day I went in there and inspected them. . . . Were we a little puckered? You probably couldn't have drove a needle up my ass with a hammer on a couple of occasions. . . . We weren't armed. . . . Sometimes guns get you in trouble.

"I got them together and told them . . . let's clean this place up. You're all going to die of Chinese Rot here. . . . [W]e were going over their records. . . . We were calling them out and making up an airplane load and shipping them out to go back to [the disciplinary barracks at] Fort Leavenworth. . . . I said, 'Now if you don't come out [when your name is called] then we're going to court-martial you for escape and you're going to get twenty more years'. . . . We just waited them out. They'd see 'Frank' go out. And 'Frank' gets on an airplane. 'Well, goddam.' Then 'Bill' goes. Then 'Joe' would shout 'I'm not going. Piss on you people.' Then they'd call out his name and he'd say, 'Here, sir.' And he'd come up front and center. . . . We never had *one* person refuse to come out. . . . It must have taken a month or so.

"We had to feed them—three meals a day. . . . They got damn C-rations. We had to give them all the water they wanted. We couldn't shut off their water or refuse to give them food. You know—the doctor and the IG [inspector general]—they were standing around like they were important.

"[We] had to rebuild everything. . . . When I went in there the fire was still smouldering. We had nothing to work with. . . . I was busy. For the first thirty days I didn't leave the stockade. Right around the clock, twenty-four hours a day. I slept right there inside the wire. When they had an alert, I wanted to be sure I was there. I had a great big baseball bat setting there. And when I went through the gate I was going to swing that sonofabitch as hard as I could. . . . We put out the fire, we started cleaning up, we tried to get the records straight . . . . We started reinforcing things. We got a goddam count. . . . Biggest thing was that the guard situation was just intolerable. Just horrible. They didn't have enough people. They were correction trained but it was a big old compound and just a boring, boring, dull job. . . . There had already been conexes but they burnt the damn place where they were. They were all inside a building built around them and burnt it down. I got these [new] conex containers and we made them into [cells] and put bars on them and put tents up over them and put them right out alongside the fence. . . . And we also cleaned up the old conexes and started filling them up again.

"We got most of the prisoners straightened out real quick and the others we just let them . . . make asses out of themselves. We put burlap on the fence around them so nobody could see them. [T]hat broke their hearts 'cause they wanted to be watched. They just kept cooling down and finally one day there was only about six or seven left. . . . They finally brought this one leader out and threw the goddam guy over the top of the goddam gate to us. . . . I think it was an argument over a damn cigarette and some C-rations. . . . They'd turn their mother in for a cigarette. . . . A lot of inmates were glad to get out of there even though they were going to Leavenworth to serve a five-year sentence.

"We told them, 'Remember, whenever you get ready to start serving your time, you just come out and knock on the door and we'll . . . lock you up and you can start all over again.'"

LIEUTENANT COLONEL TROP: "We almost had another riot.

In the compound we were moving them to, one of the guards panicked and pulled a knife .... The guard was given an Article 15 [punishment at company level] and that was all to that. I told him he was stupid for taking a knife in there but he told me he was scared."

It took a good many days for Murdock and Trop to restore order and to secure custody of the last of those prisoners who had rioted. Nearly a month after the riot, twelve inmates were still holding out in the area of the stockade they had commandeered on 29 August.

GENERAL MILDREN: "[W]hen we got down to only 13 I called my Deputy Chief of Staff for Operations and said, 'Now you go in.' We had enough tear gas there to fill New York City . . . [and also] loaded weapons. . . . These prisoners had all armed themselves. They didn't have any guns, but they had knifes and everything else that they could make out of utensils, even spears. . . . We went in and boy, there wasn't a ripple. They all held up their hands and I placed them in individual cells. Then I asked the commands to try them . . . . to take them out and try them for mutiny . . . . [I]n the first trial . . . they sentenced them to dishonorable discharge and 20 years. Then, in the next one, it was for 16 years."

It was time to calculate the cost of the riot. It had resulted in injuries to sixty-three MP personnel, including twenty-three who required hospitalization. One inmate was dead. Twenty-six needed hospital care and twenty-six others were treated as outpatients. USARV headquarters claimed that most inmate injuries were caused by prisoners hurting other prisoners. At least four inmates, and probably more, managed to escape.

Six inmates accused of starting the riot were charged with murder or conspiracy to commit the murder of the dead white prisoner. By 2 December courts-martial charges had been levied against 129 individuals for their actions during the riot: ranging from mutiny to murder, assault on a superior officer, aggravated assault, aggravated arson, simple arson, larceny, willfully destroying government property, housebreaking, and wrongful appropriation of government property.

JUDGE ADVOCATE GENERAL CAPTAIN JACK CROUCHET: "I recall very clearly that at the time the trials were going on, I thought to myself over and over how it was pure chance which brought those particular defendants to trial. In one case, a guard just happened to recognize one of the many prisoners throwing debris. The others were not accounted for. . . . The cases on which I was the Military Judge were: Cureton, Ronald. Tried on 22–23 October 1968 . . . . sentenced to 15 years, but this sentence was later reduced. . . . I thought the sentence was excessive. Coppege, David. Tried on 30 October and 9 December 1968. . . . Farmer, Samuel. Tried on 10 and 14 December 1968. Cleveland, Richard. Tried on 13 November 1968. Pleaded guilty, sentenced to 8 years, but sentence later reduced. Beauchamp, Harold K. [*sic*] Tried on 13–14 Feb[ruary] 1969. Sentenced to one year confinement at hard labor. . . Two other cases were: Frank W. Troutman. Tried on 6–7 January 1969. James M. Anthony. Tried on 3 January 1969."

JUDGE ADVOCATE GENERAL COLONEL HERBERT GREEN: "The prosecution of the riot cases was initially directed by the United States Army Vietnam Staff Judge Advocate Office . . . . They drafted all the charges and then distributed the files in each case to the General Court Martial Convening Authority of each accused. . . . Each trial counsel prepared his cases with no formal coordination with other trial counsel. . . . CID agents from throughout Viet Nam . . . interviewed prisoners, guards and other individuals who were at the scene.

"[T]he prosecution of the cases was a nightmare. . . . I could never feel entirely comfortable that I had contacted every possible witness. . . . The Article 32 investigations were held at the stockade during September-October."

Article 32 safeguards soldiers' rights. It requires that no specifications can be referred to a general court-martial for trial prior to a thorough and impartial investigation of all the charges, including an inquiry as to their truth, and whether the form of the charges is appropriate. Only after this investigation has been completed is a recommendation made whether or not to go forward with the court-martial.

An accused soldier must also be advised of all charges and of his right to be represented by counsel in the Article 32 investigation. Full opportunity is to be given to the accused to cross-examine any witnesses who will testify against him. Those requirements were followed in the prosecution of those who had rioted at LBJ.

JUDGE ADVOCATE GENERAL COLONEL GREEN: "[The] cases were then referred to trial. One case was very weak. I was satisfied that the accused was guilty but knew we had proof problems. . . . Nevertheless, we tried the case and the individual was acquitted.

"The riot was a violent action against military authority and charges of mutiny were properly alleged. However, at its core the riot was basically a severe racial incident, black against white."

Physical damages to LBJ were extensive. The mess hall was totally destroyed. The supply building, which also contained a training room, a tool room, and a mail room, was burned to the ground. Another nearby structure, the employment building, was destroyed by fire. A latrine building, referred to euphemistically by the military as a "health and comfort station," was totally destroyed. A combination shower and barber shop building was burnt to ashes, as was a supervisor's office.

The interior of the administration building was gutted, and the frame extensively damaged. Fire marshals ordered it razed, and it was pulled down on 1 September. Dozens of tents in which inmates were housed were destroyed. Total cost in 1968 dollars was $97,529. That figure, adjusted for devaluation of the dollar in the years since, would today amount to nearly one million dollars. If collateral expenses of time and equipment use by those responsible for subduing the rioters and once again bringing them under correctional control are included, the total would be staggering.

INMATE PRIVATE GREGG PAYTON: "[Authorities] knew I had been incarcerated during the riot and they felt I had knowledge of how it got started and who the organizers were. . . . So when I was in confinement after the riot [a major] comes by and wants to know what involvement I had had. Over the course of the next couple of days, I never got any real sleep. He would wake me up in my conex at different hours . . . and want to know. It hurt. He knew about pressure points of the body, so when he jab you with that stick, it was excruciating pain. You'd be woken up with a jab in the back and you'd jump up and it would be like yeah, I really want you to go off so I can really hurt you. Yeah. Go off, so I can have a good excuse for killin' you. I was truly, truly scared to death."

CONFINEMENT OFFICER LIEUTENANT COLONEL WILLIAM KEYES: "[T]ruth usually lies somewhere between what I say and I perceive and what the prisoners say and perceive. Being jabbed with a swagger stick in pressure points sounds like prisoners getting together and talking. I doubt if he knew any of the pressure points. I don't and I don't know of anyone ever teaching how to use a nightstick or swagger stick. . . . [T]hings change in time. Stories grow . . . and reputations glow."

Murdock and Trop had been assigned to LBJ on a very temporary basis. Their only task was to get control of the stockade and to reimpose custodial discipline on the inmates. That they did. Murdock was reassigned after no more than three weeks at LBJ, and Trop left for other duties only a few days later. Both were gone by 28 September.

Their replacement was the first officially designated confinement officer since the injury of Lieutenant Colonel Vernon D. Johnson on the night of 29–30 August. He was Lieutenant Colonel Ivan "the Terrible" Nelson.

# CHAPTER NINE

# ORDER RESTORED

When Lieutenant Colonel Ivan "the Terrible" Nelson arrived at LBJ in September 1968, he was well aware of the responsibility he was about to shoulder. He and his men would have to cope with a custodial nightmare. Under his leadership, they would have to deal with the long-term effects of the riot, restore inmate life to normal patterns, and rebuild LBJ into a proper working facility. They needed to clean up the rubble. Prisoners needed new housing. They had to build new operating offices for administrative personnel. They also needed new rules to govern inmate behavior and prevent a repetition of the 29–30 August riot. It was going to be a difficult job, but Nelson did not doubt his ability to succeed.

MP CLERK MIKE DOHERTY: "After the riots, the Army sent in a Patton-type ass-kicker. A small, mean-looking infantry officer. His name was Ivan Nelson and prisoners called him 'Ivan the Terrible.' He came in September and cracked down on the staff. Some were pretty lax. He got rid of [MP] potheads by bringing in other MPs and dogs to sniff. Anyone found with drugs was on his way to the front the next day. He worked us twelve hour days, six-and-a-half days a week.

"At first we thought he was just fooling around, but he wasn't. It was either his way or the highway. He started riot control training. Every night we'd get our full gear and fall into formations and practice. We worked at it until we got it down right.

"He did away with prisoner privileges. Prisoners [had] slept in tents with wooden floors. They burned these. So Ivan . . . had conex boxes sent, cut holes in them so prisoners could breathe. They were allowed out for one-half hour a day, for PT, to shower and shave. The real hard core were fed inside their conexes.

"There was no more diddly-boppin or Black Power salutes or peace signs or special handshakes. All prisoners marched or ran at all times everywhere. When they encountered an officer, they had to stop and stand at attention until the officer told them to move on.

"Ivan spent many personal hours at Big Red making sure prisoners were working and sandbags were being filled. [Guards] stopped at nothing to get control back. Nothing. Sweatboxes, PT, marching, ass-kicking. In a while [Nelson] had the stockade jumping, prisoners acted like they were in the military again. I think he did a good job."

JUDGE ADVOCATE GENERAL COLONEL HERBERT GREEN: "Under [Ivan Nelson's] command the stockade became a very strict institution. . . . [A]ny time a prisoner saw an officer he would immediately come to attention, remove his head gear, slap it against his leg and say something such as 'Prisoner Jones reports' or 'Good morning.' Prisoners were not permitted to salute officers—saluting was considered . . . a privilege . . . forfeited by those in a prisoner status. . . . Essentially, the stockade became a place where prisoners didn't blink without permission."

MP BRIGADE STAFF SECTION OFFICER O. LYNN MCCOTTER: "I have never seen a better run prison operation than what Ivan Nelson did. . . . he's the turning point. Without him they could have had a major disaster on their hands. . . . During World War II he was a stay-behind guerrilla and an advisor to Chiang Kai-shek. He started as infantry and later became MP. He was . . . in the military's airborne operations, particularly in arctic experimentation.

"Under Nelson the place became steel and barb wire; immaculate, absolute discipline. The burned stuff was pretty well cleaned up. The conex containers were in place. We called them 'Steel City,' 'Silver City.' [The place became so] well groomed you could eat off the ground. Spit and polish. Discipline. Respect. He put the place back together and on its feet. And you know? Inmates liked it. Say what you want. Those inmates had total respect for Ivan Nelson as an individual and soldier. He commanded respect. He treated everybody identically by the book. It didn't matter what your color was, what your rank had been. No favoritism. Discipline the best of any place I've ever been. Everything ran by the book."

Lieutenant Colonel Nelson did his work well. Prisoners made no new attempts at disturbing the peace of the compound. The grounds themselves once again took on the appearance of a prison rather than a war-ravaged battleground. Nelson left for a new assignment on or about 28 November 1969.

The officer who replaced Nelson after his year of duty at LBJ ended was Lieutenant Colonel William Keyes. He arrived as a promotable major, and, before taking over, pinned on his uniform the silver oak leaf rank of a lieutenant colonel. He had his own view of Ivan the Terrible. Although Keyes acknowledged that Nelson did a creditable job in a difficult situation, he saw many things that needed to be changed. Keyes offered up a lengthy comment about his actions as confinement officer and how he tried to make LBJ a more efficiently run operation, in the process correcting some of the things that Nelson and his predecessors had done.

WILLIAM KEYES: "Nelson and I never saw eye-to-eye on anything, but he was probably the right man for the time to take control.... What I meant by that was that he took control. The methods he used probably wouldn't have been the same ones I would have used.... He walked around with a chip on his shoulder at all times. Very rarely smiled.... He was MP branch but had no correctional background.... He was a strange personality.... Nelson had a real tough job.... I overlapped with him a short time until he left, and then I was able to take over and do something.... When I got there, I saw a lot of things wrong, but there wasn't a lot I could do about it til Nelson left. Nelson was a strong authority figure. He didn't share anything. I used to hear lessons from him: 'You're going to be commander here, but I'm still commander.' I felt like I was on the USS *Caine* with Captain Queeg.

"I was brand new. They were taking me around to show it to me. I went into medium security and there was a guard post and on a shelf by a window in there sat three CS [tear gas] grenades, like apples sitting in the sun. You don't have things like that inside! You keep them outside and bring them in if you need them. The prisoners were unkempt. They weren't clean. Some of these people, if left to their own devices, will never wash. There was no recreation to speak of. All they could do was walk around and talk to each other. The idea of organized sports just wasn't there. Nelson would have considered that 'coddling.'

"Before the riot inmates lived in tents, but they'd burned them. When I got there, the conexes were in place. Nelson brought them in. Couldn't burn conexes. They were publicized as 'inhumane,' but not so. It wasn't a bad idea, except he didn't go about it in the right way.... People [were] living like animals when I got there. They were [in] conexes in the medium custody Sentenced Area. They had holes in them, so they weren't sweatboxes, but there wasn't any bed, just a blanket. These [conexes] sat on the dirt, not on concrete pads. They looked like doghouses. Terrible, with a guy sitting in the corner on the floor, which was even more terrible, and I don't think there was a whole lot of effort to keep clean.

"[Then there were newer conexes.] I didn't order them built. They were in the process when I got there. I just used them.... The conexes I used had concrete pads, had every other slat taken out, painted silver because it was a color we could keep clean.... I put them under a canopy—a pole building—that reflected the sun; it was the coolest place in the stockade. It was kept clean.... Inmates had beds, books to read, magazines, had water. It doesn't seem like a real treat, but they did. Within that complex, they had showers where they could get clean every day.

"The prisoners' personal deposit fund was just a mess. The [administration] building had been burned and [inmates'] military pay certificates [had been kept there].... The money was burned and not accounted for.... They had [found only] a couple of out-of-date MPC bags that were partially burned. They didn't know whose money that was. I don't know if people ever got their money back during that period.

"When I took over, we tried to get more work for the inmates. We set up a concrete block production line. The line that made the most got to eat first. The inmates loved it. We used Big Red. Filling sandbags is a very practical thing to do in the middle of a war. There wasn't anything wrong with that. It couldn't take too many prisoners [however], so we added a little paint shop.

"I had no trustees. I had minimum custody prisoners [MCP] and parolees. An MCP goes out with an unarmed guard—a half a dozen—and worked outside. A parolee goes out by himself, to 18th Brigade headquarters, to sweep out offices and run errands. When they wanted to paint their rocks white, he did that. Why the Army always wants to paint rocks white, I don't know.

"I tried to be visible. I was in the area *all* the time. . . . Once I had control of the place I'd walk around and people . . . would talk to me . . . but I never got a single complaint about any of them getting beat. . . . I'll take a polygraph on that. . . . I used to tell [my guards], 'I can't tell the difference between one assault and another. If a prisoner assaults somebody, that's an assault. If a guard assaults a prisoner, that's an assault. And they're both court-martial offenses.'

"The biggest thing we did was to reduce the population from 650 when I got there to 250 when I left. It was so easy. . . . We set up a Correctional Holding Detachment. . . . The holding detachment worked well. Anybody with a sentence of more than thirty days became mine. He was in *my* command. I became his commander. It was a new concept. I didn't dream it up, but . . . it came down through Army channels. Someone decided it would take an administrative burden off the hands of commanders of units.

"Prior to that, anybody who was in the stockade [still] belonged to his parent unit, [often] miles away. A man would go in to pretrial confinement, which was supposed to be [only] for a limited time. He was supposed to have charges read to him within seventy-two hours, but it might take two or three weeks. Remember, the company commander was out there fighting the bad guys and trying to keep his guys alive. He's not really worried about the fellow in the stockade. He's out of his hair. Out of sight, out of mind. That guy is nothing but a bad memory to him.

"After [finally] getting the charges read, there was pretrial confinement before the court-martial. That sometimes went on for months. Quite often, by the time a guy had been there three or four months, someone would show up with a completed discharge and take him and throw him out of the Army, and he would never be tried. That's unconstitutional!

"Then also, if you got six months [punishment from a court-martial], you served six months less 'good time.' Everybody got 'good time.' Five months usually [were served] on a six-month charge. People were piling up because they weren't getting tried; because there wasn't any evaluation of prisoners. A prisoner could be in the stockade, finish his sentence, and go back to the same unit. The First Sergeant [of his old unit] would say, 'Okay, you son of a bitch. The first time you look cross-eyed you're going back to LBJ.' I know that.

"The guy had a grudge against everybody in his unit anyway, so it wasn't going to make things right to go back to the same unit. Often a man came right back to LBJ on another offense, spent *more* time in pretrial confinement, and *more* time in a sentence. Some of these guys were coming to the stockade two and three times. We had [high] recidivism—and we got that down to 8 percent. . . . A guy slugs his sergeant. It's a situational thing. The sergeant's nerves are frayed, he's being a real SOB. The kid's reached his limit and the next thing you know—BOOM—the kid's [back] in the stockade. That guy's not the same as someone who's been sitting around hating his mother and father or wanting to cut the heart out of the nearest policeman.

"I was in a war and I wanted to help. . . . I can't say I was thrilled with what I was doing over there. I'd much rather have [had] a battalion someplace where the enemy was but . . . in some instances I did some things I'm kind of proud of. . . . We couldn't bring a single soldier into Viet Nam unless one left because we had a cap on troop strength, a manpower ceiling. If we kept 650 people in that stockade, that was over a battalion that couldn't be doing their duty to help us stay alive over there. That was what pushed me.

"I went over to see the USARV's Staff Judge Advocate [officer]. . . . I told him we needed to be more efficient in getting prisoners out of there. Previous stockade commanders didn't even bother to call a prisoner's company commander. . . . With the backing of the deputy commander, USARV, I'd pick up the phone and call the CG [commanding general] of that division and say, 'I've got a guy here who's

over seventy-two hours [and no charges have been filed on him]. I'm
going to put him on report [for availability] to USARV tomorrow.'
They'd say, 'No, no,' and would run down, and the charges would
be read.

"The same thing was true on trials. I would call USARV's chief of
staff and say, 'Colonel, we're not getting what we should.' Soon I'd
get a call back telling me that somebody would be down right away.
So we were getting people tried on time. They didn't stay in pretrial
confinement a long time, which was unconstitutional as hell.

"There is a discharge called a 208—not adaptable to military service. There are people like that no matter what you do with them.
Where it used to take four or five months to process them, it [now]
took us about two or two-and-a-half weeks until I had them on an
airplane back to the States.

"Then when a man started to serve his sentence, we already had
him under observation. I had a psychiatrist, a team of psychologists
and social workers, an attorney. I finally got the people I wanted
because I ran a whole lot of NCOs out and brought in people provided me by 18th MP Brigade. I got people who were human beings.
All of a sudden the animosity inside dropped off. We took people
who were sentenced and within thirty days . . . if they had a clean
record, wanted to go back to duty, were first or second offenders
(depending on circumstances), they went back to duty . . . but not to
the same unit. We assigned them to a different major command, a
different division, sometimes a different corps area. They never went
back to the same place.

"I had a flare-up just before I left. It didn't get to a riot, but I had
some people who refused to work. I came down on them like a ton
of bricks. When they looked out [the window] there were 250 men
standing there with rifles and bayonets. . . . I went in and assembled
them and said, 'I don't have any quarrel with most of you and you
don't with me, but we've got about a dozen guys in here causing
trouble. I'm going to call their names. They're going to fall out and
I'm taking them over to maximum custody.' The sergeant called out
the first name. Abernathy, or some name that started with A. The
guy mumbles, 'I'm not going out there.' A whole bunch of voices said

'Oh, yes, you are.' So he came out. We got things pretty well settled down.

"I think I made the turnaround. I think Paul Grossheim kept it going."

Lieutenant Colonel William Keyes did not speak of one troublesome incident that he faced during his year as confinement officer, from 29 November 1968 to 28 November 1969. Much has been said here in previous pages about enlisted men who became inmates at LBJ. They were not the only ones behind the wire of the stockade. Men of higher rank also sometimes found themselves imprisoned there. A later confinement officer spoke of officers who were confined within the limits of LBJ.

LIEUTENANT COLONEL ELI GARDNER: "We had a few officer prisoners. A couple of WOs [warrant officers], a couple of lieutenants. Maybe a captain. Not many. Five or six at the most. Somebody had an SF [Special Forces] colonel, but I had no one that high. They were in for things like larceny, marijuana. They were housed separately, not made to do any work not commensurate with rank. So we gave them work like developing lesson plans or administrative work. 'Officer prisoner' is a special category. They lived in a special barracks. Not essentially different but with more privacy."

The colonel of whom Gardner spoke was Robert Bradley Rheault, in May 1969 the newly appointed commander of 5th Special Forces. He was the highest ranking person ever to spend time within the prison compound at LBJ. As a result of an incident that became highly politicized and publicized, he and six of his men were kept there: Major David Crew, Major Thomas Middleton, Captain Leland Brumley, Captain Robert Marasco, Captain Budge Williams, and Chief Warrant Officer Edward Boyle.[1]

These men were suspected of having killed an alleged Vietnamese double agent, Thai Khac Chuyen, who disappeared about 20 June 1969. General Creighton Abrams insisted on pressing charges. The accused men were arrested and brought to LBJ for pretrial confinement on 21 July 1969.

---

[1]The following account is drawn from Berry, *Those Gallant Men*, pp. 92–163 and Jeff Stein, *A Murder in Wartime* (New York: St. Martin's Press, 1992), *passim*.

They were charged not only with Chuyen's premeditated murder but with having conspired for some two weeks prior to that to murder him. Murder carried a possible death penalty. A conviction of conspiracy carried a penalty of life imprisonment. Rheault was so new to his job he had not even met some of his codefendants at the time the men were arrested.

It had begun with a CIA intelligence gathering operation disguised as a civil affairs project and was named B-57. The program, using Green Beret personnel, established agent networks in Cambodia and Laos, areas where the United States was not officially operating. The entire effort was conducted under top secret conditions. Field commanders in Viet Nam believed that information supplied by B-57 helped save American lives. Then intelligence reports began to dry up. Important agent sources suddenly died or disappeared without trace. Those involved with B-57 began to wonder who was responsible for leaking information about their efforts. The trouble was traced to Chuyen. And then he disappeared.

Little doubt exists that the Special Forces men were indeed responsible for Chuyen's death, although his body was never found. And why should they not have acted? They were in a war, and they believed they had found a traitor in their midst. It is also probable that they acted on the advice of the CIA; that is, they did so under direction of higher authority.

Nevertheless, Rheault and his men were arrested and confined at LBJ to await court-martial. Save for Rheault, who lived in an air-conditioned trailer, the men were confined in separate conex containers and forbidden to communicate with one another. The preliminary (Article 32) hearing took place on 31 July and 2 August and 20–21 August 1969 in the stockade chapel. In this discovery phase of the trial, Judge Advocate General lawyers for the Green Berets demanded the appearance of a great number of witnesses, including some from the CIA. They asked for an opportunity to look at extensive secret documents, including some from CIA files. They alleged that General Creighton Abrams, commander of USMACV, had tainted the proceedings and was using his command influence in improper ways.

The prosecution refused most of those demands. Counsel for the defense then asserted that if the government wished to keep matters secret, it could not constitutionally try the Green Berets. The only option was to drop the case. A three-week continuance of the pre-liminary hearing was granted while the Army tried to decide what to do.

The case was attracting attention and great sympathy for the Green Berets among Americans at home. Lawyers for the defense spoke out at press conferences. The media splashed details across front pages and onto television screens. Even members of Congress lobbied on behalf of the men at LBJ, and questions were raised about the conditions under which they were being held. Some public fig-ures wondered why the men had been arrested. The Army decided to let the men out of their conexes. On 20 August they were moved into a trailer on the Long Binh compound outside the wire of LBJ.

Now living outside the wire, Rheault and his men began rigorous PT training including a five-mile run each morning. They were sup-posed to be accompanied by armed MP guards, but such runs were beyond them as they would have been for most soldiers. Once basic training has been completed, there are usually few physical fitness requirements for garrison soldiers to fulfill. Stockade guards at LBJ were working twelve-hour shifts and few of them had either the time or energy to engage in long-distance running.

Physical prowess, however, was at the heart of life for those in Special Forces. Even in confinement, Rheault's men wanted to con-tinue their exercise runs. So command authority at LBJ soon allowed the Green Berets to conduct their PT exercises alone if they promised not to try to escape.

Then, for a time, authorities at LBJ and USARV became con-cerned about the security of the Special Forces prisoners. It was rumored that elsewhere In-Country, several Green Berets had begun to plot a rogue rescue mission for their imperiled fellows.

Defense lawyers continued to meet with their clients and to insist that they had a right to subpoena witnesses and evidence from the CIA. Without that information, they said, they would be unable to mount an effective defense, and any courts-martial held under such circumstances would be unconstitutional. Then, on 29 September 1969, an order suddenly came down from command authority at the Pentagon dismissing the case. The reason given was that CIA had determined "in the interest of national security" not to provide either documents or witnesses. The case was over, but the careers of seven officers had been ruined. And Chuyen was still dead.

Confinement officer William Keyes moved on to a new assignment in late November 1969, after a year at LBJ. His deputy served as confinement officer for a few days until the arrival of Lieutenant Colonel Willy Jones. Jones served only about six months as head of the prison facility before surrendering command to Lieutenant Colonel Paul Grossheim.

The stockade had been a shambles after the riot, although it had been sufficiently restored to be usable after a frantic clean-up. Rather than rebuild it entirely, United States Army Vietnam headquarters at Long Binh, acting upon recommendations from 18th MP Brigade and officials at LBJ, decided to approve construction of a new facility. Planners agreed that the old site was no longer adequate to house all the GIs sent there from the several U.S. commands within Viet Nam. They made this decision even though the total number of confinees at LBJ had dropped drastically from the days before the riot, due to the new procedures for more rapid and efficient handling of prisoners set up by Lieutenant Colonel Keyes. Orders were given. Plans were drawn up to build anew alongside the still obvious signs of the 1968 riot. Money was appropriated and set aside. Construction on the new site began during the command tenure of Keyes's successor, Willy Jones, and was completed while Lieutenant Colonel Paul Grossheim headed the LBJ facility.

The old stockade, covering 7.9 acres, was abandoned and a new one built adjacent to it, covering 5.5 acres of the massive Long Binh installation. A drug abuse holding center would take over most of the old site, with some space reserved to use as a prison overflow area. Work on the new maximum cellblock began on 28 July 1970 and was completed on 20 December 1970. Construction of the remainder of the new stockade began on 20 December 1970 and was completed on 1 July 1971. In all, the new stockade was built by the 92nd Engineer

Battalion of the 159th Engineer Group in 337 days. The facility finally became operational on 2 August 1971, although the first group of prisoners was moved from the old compound to the new one on 9 July.

The new stockade had a maximum inmate capacity of 395. It could house 120 in maximum DSEG. The medium compound could hold 175 inmates and the minimum custody compound a total of 100 inmates. Another 60 individuals could be housed in available regular troop billets outside LBJ in what the Army called a "parolee program," but that in civilian life would be referred to as a "halfway" program.

Each barracks building erected on the new compound housed up to 24 men and was equipped with overhead fans, showers, toilet, and washing facilities. The new facility cost $327,000 (or over $3,000,000 in dollars of the late 1990s). To supervise those prisoners, nine officers, two warrant officers, and 201 MP noncommissioned officers and enlisted soldiers had to be assigned to LBJ.

Briefing notes prepared later, used to inform visitors about the new facility, described the mission of the stockade: to provide for the custody and correctional treatment of military prisoners who had been ordered into confinement by proper authority. The objective of the new LBJ was "to return the maximum number of military prisoners to duty with their units as morally responsible and well-trained individuals, and to promptly identify those who [could not or would not] adjust to military [life], and return them to the United States to be further confined or discharged from the military."

Those briefing notes further stated that the labor of inmates would be used for the well-being of the Army in Viet Nam. An inmate repair and utilities program maintained the stockade in such areas as plumbing, electricity, carpentry, landscaping, painting, and masonry. A vehicle repair shop trained prisoners as mechanics. Some men painted stockade buildings while others constructed cement footers for revetments or sorted clothing or made concrete blocks or built wooden pallets. And, of course, labor at Big Red continued. There were always sandbags to fill. Other prisoners were given duty as clerks, cooks, and barbers. All this, the notes concluded, saved the government an estimated $175,000 yearly and on-the-job training prepared inmates for later eventual careers in civilian life.

There was also classroom training in both military and nonmilitary subjects. Inmates could complete high school at LBJ and General Equivalency Diploma (GED) tests were offered weekly. Even some college courses were available, and the credits so earned were accepted by several stateside colleges.

Personal counselors, chaplains, lawyers, physicians, dentists, and mental hygiene experts were all available to inmates at the new LBJ. A personnel section stored and safeguarded prisoners' valuables while they were confined. An administrative section maintained reports, records, and general paperwork necessary for day-to-day operation of the stockade. A postal section efficiently delivered mail to inmates and a supply section provided shaving materials, toothbrushes and toothpaste, writing materials, and cigarettes. An inmate-run laundry gave prisoners clean clothing and saved the expense of using outside commercial concerns. It was a self-run, self-contained stockade.

Recreational activities were available as well, ranging from basketball and volleyball to table games of all types, including table tennis. There was a reasonably well-stocked library. Prisoners could watch both television and movies shown twice weekly or seek out a crafts shop to experiment with leatherwork, carving, painting, or model building. All in all, the new LBJ was a model prison facility. Any of the fifty states back in "the World" would have been proud to claim the new confinement center as its own. The shame is that it took from 1966 to 1971 to build this appropriate facility. Had it existed years earlier, much trouble might have been avoided.

Construction of that new LBJ was completed during the tenure of Lieutenant Colonel Paul Grossheim, a confinement officer who took command on 14 July 1970 and stayed until 4 July 1971. His first few days were exciting ones.

LIEUTENANT COLONEL GROSSHEIM: "When I arrived . . . [Jones] met me at Tan Son Nhut and took me to Long Binh, got me some clothes, and took me by the place I was supposed to sleep. . . .

about a block and a half from the prison. . . . Told me to get a good night's sleep. . . . The next morning I got up and there was no other officer around. Just deserted. I didn't really know where the prison was or the dining room. I got dressed and started walking down the road. By the time I was closer, I could see Military Police dressed in riot gear, gas masks, and fixed bayonets, surrounding the stockade. I was able to get inside, found this Jones, and said, 'What's going on?' 'We're having a little disturbance,' he replied. 'Well, gee, it would have been nice if you had told me. I would like to have seen how you handled it.' His response was, 'We wanted you to have a good night's sleep because you'll probably have your [problems] real soon'. . . . He left [for a new assignment] the same day or the next day. That was my initiation to that facility.

"Shortly afterwards, I walked around the entire place to see what was going on, and I was told by inmates and NCOs that they weren't used to having the confinement officer walk through. . . . That Jones was right. About three days later there was another little disturbance. About five days later there was another. Then instead of having about one a week, it was every two weeks. Then once a month. Then once every other month. By January [1971], after I had been there six months, we never had another incident. The disturbances were inmates assaulting other inmates, inmates barricading themselves into buildings, piling up all the furniture so you couldn't get in there, some setting of fires. None that involved loss of life."

An MP supply clerk remembered some of the differences between the old and new jails.

SPECIALIST FOURTH CLASS KEN COWAN: "When I got there in [March] '71 the new part was [still] under construction. Four months after I got there they switched over to the new jail. . . . The new stockade was better. . . . It was built to be a state-of-the-art kind of thing. People started turning themselves in who had been AWOL for a long time—one guy for five years in Saigon. The new LBJ was more lax in its treatment of inmates, a lot more professional. The war's nearly over. We're all in the same predicament. You got to play the game. You got to go to jail but you'll be okay. Whatever you did, the Army made you do it."

MP GUARD JOHNNY COURTHERS: "When I got there [in June 1971] we were still using the old Long Binh compound. We moved into the new stockade a few months later. It was a much better facility. Better guard towers. The inside was very nice. The general population stayed in dormitories, like barracks. It was kept clean and spotless.

"I worked guard tower, inner gates, front gate. All I did was to open and close and lock the gates when there was movement of personnel through them, or when supplies would come in. I also worked as a counselor for a time. . . . We worked long hours. Twelve on, twelve off. The day started about 6 A.M. When we were off duty we could go to a Chinese restaurant on post, a massage parlor on post. . . . The prisoners were regular guys, most of them. I even met one or two I had grown up with. I learned a long time ago it's a small world."

MP NONCOMMISSIONED OFFICER IN CHARGE (NCIOC) CLIFFORD PROSSER: "I worked at the new concrete block facility. . . . The new block could be compared to a present-day county jail. Had a little basketball [court], recreational area, even flush toilets in each cell, unbreakable polished aluminum mirrors on walls. Bunks were plywood with a mattress on top. The toilets cut down on the smell that was at Silver City. The only time I had occasion to work in Silver City was one time we had a near riot and had to go into the compound and we used the old Silver City for overage in detention. I was there a little while then and, God, I couldn't believe they had actually used that place.

"Because it was a tropical country, the cell blocks were semi-open. They were screened; the cells were in an inner block and you could walk around them on the entire perimeter, about thirty cells, on a walkway.

"There were two buildings on each side of the compound, generally facing each other, with an office building in between. Four identical cell blocks, fifteen on a side, thirty cells in each building with a small office in front where we did our paperwork, and a central office where the lieutenant and NCOIC of the compound stayed. Then each cell block had an E-5 NCIOC.

"I had worked in maximum security at Fort Sill and when I went to Viet Nam I volunteered for that at LBJ.... The reason I was NCOIC after having been in service less than two years was that 95-C MOSs [confinement specialists] were so new they needed to make NCOs [of us] in a hurry. Rank came pretty fast. If I remember right, I was a PFC [only] nine days. I was a SP-5 [specialist fifth class] after nine months of service. I was NCOIC of cell block Number 3, the 'ghetto'.... It was called the 'ghetto' because I had the bad guys, men that killed their COs [commanding officers] and stuff like that. Fragging was a big thing over there. If your squad leader wasn't a good one you just got rid of him, rolled a grenade under his bunk or whatever. We had several guys who had done that. My block was supposed to be the problem prisoners, the disciplinary prisoners.

"And, of course, 'ghetto' has cultural implications. Ethnic parallels. Ninety percent, probably 98 percent of my prisoners were black. There was a real strong racial undertow in the country in general. And it was certainly true in the stockade. In the general prison population ... maybe six out of ten were black.

"Most of our prisoners were in for homicide; a lot of druggers. Several of my prisoners were officers in the Black Panther Party. Lots of deserters/AWOLs staying in Saigon. Unless it was all sham, blowin' smoke, there was Panther activity in Saigon.

"There wasn't much difference between us and the prisoners ... in maximum security. We were all in there, pretty isolated from everything else. We worked twelve-hour shifts and from seven to fifteen or sixteen days without a day off. It got pretty isolated."

An inmate gave his thoughts both about life at the new LBJ and about the continuing war in Viet Nam. A Native American and full-blooded Navajo, he had been adopted at the age of two months and given the name Paul F. Throckmorton. In later years he chose for himself the name given here.

INMATE PRIVATE CY SKYHORSE: "I was at both the old and new stockades. Living in the new stockade was like the Hilton. Native American warriors went to Viet Nam without question with the idea they were defending their homeland, but when we got there we saw that the Vietnamese had skin like ours. It was genocide. I met another

Native American warrior at LBJ, a Cherokee from Oklahoma named Barnett. He had walked point for his unit. Many Native American warriors walked point."

But troubles at LBJ never really ended. Finding it harder now to complain about the facility itself, prisoners could always vent their frustrations on each other.

INMATE PRIVATE ROBERT JACKSON: "[In the summer of 1971 at the new LBJ] we had a riot over the whites making fun of the blacks doing 'Daps,' where they went through this little hand slap-ping/knocking thing that usually was associated with the Black Power/Malcolm X-type stuff. About fifty blacks stormed our bar-racks early one evening. . . . [A] forty-man riot squad came in full gear and used Mace and clubs to end the thing, but only using them on the blacks. . . . The riot squad . . . automatically assumed [the blacks] were the cause since they'd barricaded themselves into one of the barracks. They tear-gassed the barrack and used liquid Mace and nightsticks on them until they were all outside laying on the ground and totally subdued. They were free with Mace and clubbed anyone who was standing after the order to file out and assume a prone position on the ground.

"The riot only lasted about an hour before it was completely squashed. . . . They ended up locking every black in the compound in solitary and had to open the old section of Silver City to accommo-date them all. Then a colonel came in and they formed the whites up on the exercise yard while this colonel explained that he knew we hadn't tried to fight or tear anything up but that the Niggers were hollering that they were being prejudiced [against] and would we all go ahead and go to solitary for a few days, too, so the Niggers wouldn't have any more to complain about. We all went."

Sometimes, it seemed, inmate complaints and consequent de-mands were trivial and insignificant. They wore down the patience of the administration. An inmate at LBJ during April, May, and June 1971, while Paul Grossheim served as confinement officer, told of one such episode when black prisoners began to riot.

INMATE PRIVATE TERRY SMOOT: "The colonel came out to talk to them. I had the feeling that if they had tried to be reasonable, he'd have tried to accommodate them, but they asked for things like a color TV in their hooch. I don't believe at the time there was a single one in Vietnam. So the colonel just kind of shook his head and said [to the guards]: 'Gas 'em.'"

LIEUTENANT COLONEL GROSSHEIM: "One of the things I did shortly after assuming command was to stop bringing in rifles with fixed bayonets to quell a disturbance. . . . I changed . . . to long MP batons . . . four feet long . . . and we used those . . . and they were very successful because [while] inmates were aware that MPs might not be willing to shoot or stab them, they were very skilled with the use of clubs. Used as an extension of the arm, holding them in front and making jabs. Generally you jab toward the stomach or the ribs and the force is enough to get someone's attention. . . . That worked very well."

Even in the new facility, personnel shortages continued to be a problem. There never seemed to be enough trained men available to serve in the stockade. Sometimes they could be found elsewhere performing other MP duties.

LIEUTENANT COLONEL GROSSHEIM: "I was able sometimes to divert NCOs I had known previously on other assignments. . . . They knew how to handle prisoners. They had a vast knowledge of working with troubled soldiers and what to expect from me. . . . They were very well schooled in how to do prison counts, in how to talk to an inmate without getting him excited, how to do shakedown inspections, how to put on hand and leg irons."

Hand and leg irons? Those tools might evoke images of medieval days and dungeons rather than of a modern, humane correctional facility. Yet such manacles were used at LBJ and they are still used in American jails for specific occasions: to transport an unruly prisoner between two points to ensure safety both for the prisoner and his guards, and as a temporary restraining method to keep an inmate from harming either himself or others.

LIEUTENANT COLONEL GROSSHEIM: "I got many capable people . . . but they had never worked inside a prison before. . . . Then when you'd get short of people . . . we'd go to the replacement company and anyone who came in with a Military Police skill was sent [to USARVIS] or [even] infantry people who didn't know which way was up. [We] often times placed [them] inside the facility . . . in the towers, arm them with weapons, and that didn't cause a problem. But if they were already on drugs from their experience in combat, . . . they'd be drug users when they came to the facility and so that didn't work out well.

"Often times I had as many as two shipments [of inmates back to the States] a week, anywhere from ten to eighteen at a time. . . . They went back on the same airplanes that brought new troops to Viet Nam. I got rosters of combat units around Long Binh and it was my custom to put one good guy with two inmates. If I had a shipment of ten there would be at least five good soldiers going and usually a senior NCO and, in some cases, an officer.

"Escort guard was selected as one of the benefits of being 'soldier of the week' or 'soldier of the month' or something outstanding in combat. Units would volunteer these people to take trips back as guards. . . . It gave them a chance to get home for a visit. . . . I even let privates and PFCs and corporals go on them, so this added to their morale."

Chaplain (Major) Wayne King spent his year in Viet Nam as Grossheim's religious leader at LBJ, and the colonel worked more closely with his chaplain than had his predecessors. King remembered those days vividly. He recalled one of the ways used by Grossheim to control inmates.

CHAPLAIN KING: "There was this guy ready to go back to [the States] . . . . In order to get on the plane [inmates] had to get a haircut and wear a nice uniform. I was down at max security and this guy said he wasn't going to get his hair cut. I . . . heard [the colonel] say, 'Well, if you don't want to get your hair cut, you're not going to go back. Just keep you here. No problem'. . . . The guy was mad, but he finally agreed . . . . He had the biggest Afro I've ever seen. He [also] hadn't shaved. The colonel said, 'No problem, if he doesn't shave, he doesn't eat.' The guy was a mess. The colonel said [to me], 'Why generate problems?'"

The legend of LBJ as the worst place to be in all Viet Nam continued, but the reality had become far different. Newly constructed on a different site, the stockade had become a far different facility than it had been in earlier years. Living conditions for inmates had improved. Overcrowding was no longer a problem. Guards were better trained. There were fewer complaints about mistreatment. Prisoners were processed more quickly and efficiently. Their courts-martial occurred with fewer delays, and men no longer spent endless days in pretrial lockup. Following their sentences, when possible, they were soon sent either to new units within Viet Nam or to longterm confinement back in the States.

All these measures were an improvement. They helped officials at LBJ to deal with the steady stream of men in trouble with military law who continued to arrive at the front gate.

# CHAPTER TEN

# BACK TO THE BEGINNING

The job of military chaplain officers has a built-in tension. Their position is that of staff officer to the commander for religion, morals, and morale. They regularly brief their bosses on those matters. They also lead worship services and provide opportunities for those of other faiths in their units to receive the religious ministrations of their own rites. And they serve as counselors and confessors to troubled soldiers who need religious or general counseling. In a sense they are commissioned to be a friend to enlisted personnel, to help their soldiers in any way they can. Soldiers know that chaplains are the only officers they can always count on when they face difficulties. Troops know with certainty that chaplains, to whom they pour out their troubles, will always respect their confidences and privacy. This status is protected by Army Regulations. Chaplains are an important and integral part of military life. Their guidance has often made a real difference in the lives of those with whom they work.

Chaplain Wayne King's introduction to life as a chaplain at LBJ abruptly acquainted him with the intensity of the place. He arrived on 2 August 1970, only a few days after Grossheim's 14 July change of command.

CHAPLAIN KING: "The first day I arrived I had the usual briefing, went to my hooch outside the wire. It was Saturday night so I prepared my sermon for the next day. It was pouring down rain and I finally went to bed. [Later] I hear this beating on my door. I opened it and there stood my two assistants. 'Chaplain King, there's a riot in the stockade.' I thought 'So? What am I supposed to do?' 'You're supposed to go to the stockade.' So I put my rain jacket . . . and my soft cap on and we ran up the two blocks to the stockade.

"I asked my assistant 'What am I supposed to do?' 'Well, you're supposed to be with the colonel.' We ran into the sally port. Guards are lined up on both sides with their steel pots, flak jackets, Mace, gas masks, and billy clubs. They're standing there. We go through. [Someone called out] 'Where are you guys going?' 'To the colonel. Where is he?'

"'The riot's in the detained compound. That's where the colonel is.' We ran there. Asked the guard where the colonel was. 'Oh, he's out in the middle of the courtyard.' So they open the gate and I go in— with fear and trepidation—and I go up to the colonel. . . . and he's in his steel pot, flak jacket, gas mask on his hip talking to these guys and they're yelling at him. I say, 'Sir! I'm here.' And he said, 'Good, chaplain. I want you to go over and talk to those guys over there.'

"Sent me down the way to talk . . . and I didn't know what to say. I was scared to death because he and I are the only two cadre-type people in the compound [and] there's a riot going on. Nobody's hitting anybody but they're angry. So I talked to the guys for awhile and then went back over to where the colonel was. He was still talking to some of them. Then he reached out and said, 'I want you, you, you, and you to follow me. We're going to max[imum disciplinary segregation]!' Then he said to me, 'Chaplain, you follow me. You take up the rear.' I was scared to death because they could do *anything* to us. Those five guys followed. Was I afraid? I was afraid at that time. After that I was not afraid of anybody at any time."

Colonel Grossheim believed his chaplain to be a competent member of his team. He recalled one of the reasons he felt that way.

COLONEL GROSSHEIM: "I remember one [incident]. I called out a reaction force and we got into riot formation with gas masks on and our gas dispenser up front and moved into the pretrial compound where this was occurring. The doors were barricaded . . . so we couldn't get in. I told the inmates to give up and come out as they had thirty seconds before we fired gas in. I heard the voice of my Chaplain, [Wayne] King, from inside saying, 'Don't do that. I've got everything under control.' There he was in there talking to inmates . . . getting them all calmed down. So we never had to dispense any gas."

Serious problems at LBJ persisted, at the new stockade as at the old one, difficulties that Colonel Grossheim did not refer to in his interview. They became public through the work of an extremely bright young man assigned to the chaplain section at LBJ. An article entitled "The Last Days of LBJ" appeared in the 10 January 1972 *Overseas Weekly,* covering events of the previous year at the jail. The writer was Specialist Fourth Class Dennis E. Hensley, a chaplain's assistant at the stockade who drew on his own experience in writing the article. He served as assistant both to Chaplain King and to his successor, Chaplain (Major) Vernon Swim. He worked at the jail while both Grossheim and his successor, Lieutenant Colonel Eli Gardner, held the position of confinement officer.

Hensley told how in "the middle of March [1971] . . . a young black prisoner named Collie Johnson had used his bedsheet to hang himself in his cell. The Army was spending $1.6 million to build an entirely new stockade one block away from the old . . . LBJ. The first section to be completed was the maximum security area . . . . This section was put into immediate use. Collie Johnson christened this new wing one night at 2 A.M. by tying a sheet to the top cell bar and then jumping off the toilet seat. . . . [T]he stockade's mental hygiene section had analyzed him as a potential suicide case. Someone had slipped. . . . One of the prisoners we had seen several times [at the chapel] for counseling was Ajary Roberts. Roberts helped keep the new wing in the headlines in the days following Johnson's suicide.

"In his first week there Roberts did what was supposed to be impossible: he escaped from maximum security by smashing a gate lock after slipping out of an exercise formation. Our patrols failed to bring him in, even though the underground word was that anyone bringing Roberts back, dead or alive, would be on the next roster for shipping prisoners back to the mainland, which included a five-day layover in Honolulu. . . . Grossheim . . . was put under immediate pressure. . . . During May and June, many steps were taken to revise the LBJ program—and reputation. . . . [O]n the May 17, 1971 roster there were over 480 prisoners. By the end of May the figure was just under 500. In August, under correctional Officer Lt. Col. Eli Gardner, at the new LBJ, the figure was always below 400."

Hensley continued. Grossheim was to leave LBJ for another assignment on 4 July 1971. The men of the 284th MP Battalion were planning to give him a surprise party the evening before he left. They were upstaged by LBJ's inmates in the Detained Compound. "At 8 P.M. the night of July 1, a race riot broke out in Detained Compound. Barracks Two ignited with fist fights between whites and blacks and quickly spread to the other two barracks on either end. From out of hidden spots came broomhandles, razor blades and various bludgeoning instruments the inmates had stored for such a time. In a matter of minutes prisoners were in fierce battle among themselves. Emergency calls were sounded for all available stockade personnel. . . . The night shift alone was not able to [contain] the riot, however, two guards were successful in rescuing three severely mauled prisoners who were immediately rushed to the 24th Evacuation Hospital emergency room. . . . As quickly as the riot had started, it ended. Not one prisoner was struck by a guard . . . . Most of the prisoners proved submissive once the futility of their efforts was seen . . . . [Major] Pederson [the deputy commander] ordered that all instigators were to be 'put in the box' (locked up in maximum security). By 10 P.M. Detained Compound was vacant."

CHAPLAIN SWIM: "My chaplain's assistant, who went on to get his doctorate, Dr. Dennis Hensley . . . wrote an article on LBJ for the *Overseas Weekly* . . . . [a] two-page spread. I lost him as a result of it. He was keeping notes for the article in a book in the chapel library. A prisoner picked the book up and took it back to his area to read it. They had a prisoner inspection, found that book, thumbed through it, and found Hensley's notes. I got called into the commander's office. 'We have evidence your assistant is writing an article about Long Binh Jail.' 'I have no idea what you're talking about.' He told of finding the notes. 'By tomorrow, I want him gone.' So I lost an excellent chaplain's assistant. Sure enough, the day he flew out of Viet Nam to go back to the U.S., the story appeared in the *Overseas Weekly*."

Lieutenant Colonel Paul Grossheim's year at LBJ ended on 4 July 1971. His successor had not yet arrived, so Grossheim turned the reins of administration over to his deputy, Major James Pederson. The major ran the stockade for a little more than three weeks, from 5 July to 29 July. On 30 July, Lieutenant Colonel Eli Gardner began his tenure as confinement officer. He served at LBJ until 8 July 1972. Colonel Gardner was the man who sent Dennis Hensley home from his job as chaplain's assistant.

Gardner was a forceful man. One of his chaplains described him.

CHAPLAIN SWIM: "[Our] new commander [was] a big black fellow who had played college football. A huge man. Spoke with as much authority as his physical image gave out."

He was the first black confinement officer, but certainly not the first African American who had served on the staff at LBJ. They were there from the beginning and at nearly all levels, from deputy confinement officer to clerks to guards in disciplinary segregation. The number of blacks on staff and the role they played at LBJ are often forgotten in tales of the so-called racism that many inmates believed they suffered during their days of imprisonment at LBJ.

Richard Nixon became president of the United States in 1968. He had long been a fervent "cold warrior" since his days as a member of the House of Representatives. He had once urged American intervention to bolster French efforts in Indochina. He regularly supported the policies of John F. Kennedy and Lyndon Johnson in Viet Nam. However, in the election campaign of 1968, when he ran for his first term of office as president, sensing the mood of war weariness in the nation, Nixon spoke of a plan to end the conflict in Viet Nam. He pledged to end the war on "honorable terms" and bring home both American fighting men and the nation's prisoners of war. At the time he spoke, U.S. troop strength was at about 550,000 men.

In June 1969, President Nixon announced his program of "Vietnamization" that would allow the United States to step back from active participation in the war. The U.S. would turn over to the Army of the Republic of Viet Nam major charge of the contest there, backed by American air power. In August, 25,000 U.S. soldiers came home. More followed. In April 1970 the president told the nation that

Vietnamization and phased withdrawal of U.S. troops were both proceeding according to plan. But even as the United States withdrew from Viet Nam, some American GIs there continued to be sentenced to Long Binh Jail. Those sent there after July 1971 found that the policies that governed their lives were now set by Eli Gardner.

LIEUTENANT COLONEL GARDNER: "When I took over it was a real command. Six or seven hundred prisoners plus the company of about two hundred and fifty people—a good, solid battalion-sized command. . . . under the [18th MP] brigade. . . . I had battalion command authority over everybody; field grade Article 15 jurisdiction, whatever court-martials I wanted to recommend. It was a great set up . . . . A lot of people miss the point on a stockade. . . . The stockade served a good purpose of getting problem people away from the combat mission. . . . The thing is, you got to treat a guy right . . . . like a soldier. You don't lose your soldier status as a prisoner. I thought that was very important. . . . You treated them like a soldier. No one was inhumane but there were areas where you could emphasize that this guy was still a soldier. That was good corrective operations.

"A stockade is a psycho-sociological operation. It's [run by] technique. . . . Keep the place on an even keel. A guy in a stockade always thinks no one cares anything about him. So I always used to watch the food because that's always a trouble source. Make sure if a guy wanted seconds he could get them. A little thing that avoids big things. I set myself up as a judge or arbitrator. A guy has to feel that when something happens there's someplace to turn to; that there's justice in the system. So we didn't have any major incidents. . . . A minor fistfight with maybe two people, but nothing serious. . . . You always have minor incidents with someone saying, I don't feel like going to work or something like that. What you do is to go in and take quick action and it's over with in seconds. That's routine running of a stockade.

"Westmoreland came down when he was chief of staff. We got a lot of pats on the back. We had a lot of good programs. . . . a work program to keep people busy.

"We started some classes with my officers as teachers—crime

prevention and black history as I recall—to the inmates. Education programs. . . . It was on a volunteer basis but we had a goodly number attend. . . . We got some washing machines that somebody had down at Cam Ranh Bay and started washing our own clothes. Kept our clothes clean. A laundry detail. We built revetments for helicopters. Built concrete blocks and filled sandbags. We started a basketball program there. My officers were the officials. That worked out pretty good. . . . The compound that wins gets to eat first. . . . The idea is to get everybody to participate. . . . We had a parolee barracks. A guy's on his own. He reports for work outside, just like a duty soldier. He goes to work, stays on duty, comes back from duty, goes back to his barracks."

In this recounting, Gardner seemingly recalls achievements made during his own tenure as confinement officer. Every confinement officer interviewed for this story did the same thing. Each one seemed to feel that he was responsible for real improvements. Gardner here is telling what he did that made a difference in the operation of LBJ. Education? One wonders, what happened to the education programs started by Keyes and Grossheim of which they were so proud? Work programs? They had existed for several years prior to his arrival. Laundry? Earlier briefing notes spoke of an inmate-run laundry service already in place. What happened to it? Games? Other confinement officers had spoken of starting basketball games. Why did Gardner have to re-invent the wheel? Parolee barracks? They had been in place for some time.

LIEUTENANT COLONEL GARDNER: "I made it a point to talk to every guy who came in. I was assessing what I had here. I was assessing the type of individual, spotting those who would be a potential problem. . . . It was very important for them to come to . . . the commander of the facility. I told them two things that kept down incidents. One was . . . you're not in Alabama now, here you are. This is the life-style here. If a man stands on his own, he gets treated equally. Two: today you're in the stockade as a prisoner. Tomorrow you and I are fighting out of the same foxhole. Don't forget that. I thought that might make an impact.

"I hate to sound boastful but the word is out that we ran a helluva stockade because of a lot of things that *didn't* happen. Everybody loves a quiet stockade. The best one in the world is one over there you didn't even know was there. We thought we ran a pretty quiet stockade. That meant working on a lot of little details. You never know which one prevented a big incident."

Colonel Gardner's chaplain, Major Vernon Swim, remembered his year of service at LBJ. He recalled certain incidents.

CHAPLAIN SWIM: "The difference between the two facilities was night and day. . . . The new facility was *so* nice the prisoners tended to foul up the day before they were to be released so they wouldn't have to go back to a unit and get shot at. They'd stay there in that cozy cell. Even maximum confinement was very nice compared to the old LBJ.

"The chapel at the new facility was so nice we always had a full chapel with people standing. I used to be complimented that they thought so much of my preaching. Then I found out that we had eight air conditioners [running], and it was the coolest place in the whole prison. Staff, prisoners, everyone, would come for the service. It was a gathering place whether there was a service going on or just a place to spend free time.

"At old LBJ they had a number of sit-down strikes, but at the new LBJ while I was there we had only one, shortly after I got there. . . . I was in [the commander's] office one day when one of his officers came in and said, 'Sir, we've got a problem. A sit-down strike. They're refusing to go to work.'

"He grabbed his hat, opened the door—WHAM—and walked out to where the guys were sitting down. As he approached, they started standing—just the way he walked, they knew it was time. He had [a] very few words with them and then they marched off to work. He was a frightening sight to behold as he marched toward those prisoners.

"When they opened the new facility, a lot of high-ranking officers and VIPs would come through to see the new facility—a showplace. They had a *nice* dining facility and a lot of people would stop in to eat their meals. I was in there one day. I'd go back in the kitchen to watch the prisoners fixing meals, although of course they were supervised.

One day I was back there and one of the guys says, 'Now chaplain, any time you eat here, you need to stand back awhile and see what the prisoners eat and what they don't eat.' 'What do you mean?' 'Well, we always sabotage something. Like today we masturbated in the mashed potatoes.' I couldn't eat mashed potatoes after that for a long time. That was their way to get back at the establishment, the officers, who were eating there.

"When you visited [maximum] security you never knew what you were going to get. Someone would take a leak on you. They'd hear you coming and be standing there waiting on you. Chaplains too! Or bad mouth you. But I met a big black guy in the first cell on one side who was kind of in charge of that place. That's the way those things are. Somebody has the power. . . . I made friends with him, so anytime I came through, he'd say, 'Okay, you guys, shape up, the chaplain's comin' through.' I never had any more problems while he was there."

The year 1972 came to an end, and so, finally, did American involvement. Almost all U.S. soldiers had been withdrawn from Viet Nam. Installations and equipment built by the United States everywhere In-Country were turned over to the southern Vietnamese government. The last confinement officer at LBJ was Captain William L. Hart, who in the years that followed went on to become the commandant at the U.S. Army Disciplinary Barracks at Fort Leavenworth, Kansas.

CAPTAIN HART: "LBJ was turned over to [the Vietnamese] in mid-February [1973]. . . . When I was there, as a captain, I was the senior officer at Long Binh, if you can believe that. Everything had moved to MACV [Military Assistance Command, Vietnam, in Saigon] from USARV [United States Army, Vietnam, in Long Binh] headquarters. . . . My point of contact was Captain Anh. He was difficult to get hold of. The Vietnamese officers were very aloof. . . . I had trouble contacting him because he was always taking a nap or going up to ARVN headquarters. I finally did contact him there. It was in the old USARV headquarters building. The Vietnamese had taken it over. . . . The Vietnamese had the darn air conditioning on full blast. It was 57 degrees in there one day! They were all running around in field jackets. . . . When I finally got hold of Anh by going through a Vietnamese colonel, I said, 'We've got to get together and establish a date for the turnover.' Then they had to have an inspection; they looked at the facilities and wanted us to repair some of them. I believe there were some cracked toilet lids and things like that. Then the actual hand-off of the facility [came]. By that time we had moved the confinees to Pershing Field in Saigon.

"The Vietnamese turned LBJ into a drug rehabilitation facility for their people. I remember we took all the pews and the bell out of the chapel and took them to a village near Bien Hoa made up of North Vietnamese refugees who had come down in 1954. They had a church but they didn't have any pews or a bell. The priest was saying Mass for us on Sundays and so I got permission to let him have the furnishings from the chapel. We loaded them on a deuce and a half and a trailer. I remember as we were going to the village—this was about two weeks after 27 January 1973 and the truce was supposed to be in effect—along the main road there, I looked to my left and here's a doggone South Vietnamese battalion maneuvering in an open space. I looked over to my right and here's a North Vietnamese regiment, and we were right slam in the middle and they were firing over our heads. . . . They exchanged artillery over our heads and we didn't have a scratch on us!

"We had constructed a temporary confinement facility using the handball courts at Pershing Field near Tan Son Nhut Air Base in Saigon to hold prisoners until the departure of U.S. forces. We were co-located with the Headquarters of the 716th Military Police Battalion, and we actually held prisoners in the compound until around the 27th of March, when the LBJ guards took the last of the prisoners back to CONUS [continental United States].

"The last few months . . . we had all corrections-trained people. As a result of that we had absolutely no incidents whatsoever. In Viet Nam, nobody even showed up positive on a drug urinalysis and no assault incidents. One guy went on a hunger strike for twenty-four hours and that was the extent of all the problems we had with the prison population. We had some really bad guys in there. We had murderers and fraggers and kidnappers, but no problems. That kind of prisoner was all we had by that time, people who had committed a serious crime. The others were detained in unit areas.

"I left Viet Nam on the last day. After General [Fred] Weyand flew out and had been airborne for one or one-and-a-half hours, there were thirty-seven of us who left on an aircraft. We were a core staff for MACV. If the general had decided to turn around and come back, he could have set up operations again. I was provost marshal at that time along with a first lieutenant and about ten MPs; plus there was a personnel guy, an operations guy, and a logistics guy—all on the C-141 that finally flew us out. We left from Camp Alpha at Tan Son Nhut about 1800 [6 P.M.] in the afternoon on 29 March 1973."

PROVOST SERGEANT FRANK WOOTEN: "I got to USARVIS in May '72 and left in March 1973. Ten months and twenty days. . . . I was the senior NCO there in the last days, the Provost Sergeant. Bruce Nagle was there, Bill Hart was there, I was there . . . the only old-timer.

"The last days were very boring. As troops left, the post of Long Binh was turned over exclusively to ARVN. We were the only American unit left. There was absolutely no support left on the base, and our prisoner population was down into the thirties. In late '72 we [the MPs] all moved inside the stockade; that became *our* compound and we moved all the prisoners into the old segregation area. We didn't treat them like segregation prisoners. They were able to live with their doors open in an open compound.

"We decided to do that on our own. Bill [Hart] and I made that decision on our own, for our own protection, our own security. . . . Nobody spoke the [Vietnamese] language much and the post was crawling with Vietnamese and even though they were regulars and allied soldiers, what can I say? We felt better going inside the wire where we had tower and fence security. We were locked in all the time. Or else they were locked out.

"The prison population fluctuated during my year there. When I arrived it was about six hundred. Instead of sending people to the stockade as things squeezed down, units sent them to the States for court-martial and sentencing. In the time I was there [the population] dropped from several hundred down to—at the very end—one in a detention cell.

"In early '73 we closed that sucker out and moved back to Pershing Field in Saigon . . . and opened up a little detention facility there. . . . Probably [had] about thirty-five [inmates] by the time we moved from Long Binh. All we did [with the prisoners] was transfer them out, get them on a plane with guys who were DEROSing [returning to the United States] who acted as guards on the way back. BAM! They got stuck with escort duty."

And so it ended. The last of the guards gone. The final prisoners transferred back to facilities in the United States. Once again Vietnamese could claim two tracts of land for their own use. One was the sprawling compound at Long Binh. In after years Vietnamese families lived in the LBJ compound and called it home. Fences were taken down. Usable materials were salvaged, dismantled, and used in ways not foreseen by the builders of both the old and the new LBJ. Small gardens dotted the area. Little children ran playing down Hall Road and sat on top of ancient American battalion area markers. The place was hardly recognizable as a former American correctional institution.

The other tract of land reclaimed by the Vietnamese was Pershing Field. In 1989, as I rode in an automobile between Tan Son Nhut airport and downtown Saigon (Ho Chi Minh City), it was impossible to locate those tennis courts. The driver had never heard of them or of the Pershing Field facility. New buildings have been erected as the country tries to cope with a population that has grown from 16,000,000 in 1954 to 70,000,000 today. Perhaps that old American stockade lies buried beneath their foundations. But both places remain firmly fixed in the minds of those who were there.

GUARD SERGEANT CLIFFORD PROSSER: "After I'd been on the Birmingham police force about five years, I was downtown about five o'clock one evening standing on a corner working a foot beat. This guy came up and said, 'Don't I know you? Wasn't you in Nam with me?' 'Mebbe I was. You look familiar.' It turned out he was a prisoner at LBJ. I recognized his face. I said, 'Yeah. I remember you.' And he said, 'Yeah. I remember you, too!'"

CHAPLAIN WAYNE KING: "LBJ was a necessary part of the war. You had to have something to take care of the really bad guys that you couldn't do anything else with."

The United States Army Vietnam Installation Stockade (USARVIS) began at Pershing Field in 1965 and ended there in 1973. It started as a small facility and finished as one. In between, at Long Binh, that sprawling detention center gained a horrific reputation as the most hated place in the war zone. It served as a deterrent for some GIs, reminding them to refrain from behavior that might cause them to end there. During its years of service it also housed thousands upon thousands of others for whom a deterrent warning was insufficient. LBJ reformed some. For a few, time spent there as inmates marked a turning point in their lives. Having broken military law, they determined that never again would they commit an act that might send them back behind bars. For the American military, it served as a place to house problem soldiers away from the combat mission, so their actions and activities would not harm or infect other soldiers.

Sadly and unfortunately, for all too many others, days spent behind the fences of USARVIS marked the beginning of a lifelong criminal record. So many of those interviewed for this study were again behind bars, locked away from society for one reason or another. Some staff members, both officers and noncommissioned officers, found they enjoyed the challenges of working in law enforcement and penal institutions and have continued to do so after leaving the military. Whichever way their lives went they would always remember the Long Binh Jail.

# THE INTERVIEWEES

BENSINGER, GARY. St. Johns, Michigan. Letter, Bensinger to Currey, 25 May 1990.

BERMAN, GLORIA J. Clinical social worker, Massachusetts Treatment Center, Bridgewater, Massachusetts. Interviewed 13 February 1990 and letter, 5 March 1990.

CHILDRESS, JIMI. Kansas State Prison, Lansing. Interviewed 9 May 1990.

COURTHERS, JOHNNY. Birmingham, Alabama. Interviewed 11 March 1990.

COWAN, KEN. Cobb, California. Interviewed 29 April 1990.

CROUCHET, JACK. Denver, Colorado. Interviewed 24 September 1990. Letter and enclosures, 13 October 1990.

CURREY, DENNIS W. Wolf Creek, Montana. Letter, 14 September 1998.

CY SKYHORSE [PAUL F. THROCKMORTON]. Leavenworth, Kansas. Letter, 12 November 1990 and interviewed 28 February 1991.

DERINGER, GEORGE. Augusta, Georgia. Letter, 29 November 1990.

DOHERTY, MICHAEL. Philadelphia, Pennsylvania. Interviewed 21 February 1990.

EASLEY, PAUL. Atlanta, Georgia. Interviewed 15 February 1990.

FOUAD, CLAUDE K. Jacksonville, Alabama. Interviewed 14 September 1990.

FORT, NATHANIEL, JR. Sanford, Florida. Interviewed 11 March 1990.

GAUL, MICHAEL T. Seattle, Washington. Interviewed 20 January 1991.

GARDNER, ELI. Columbus, Georgia. Interviewed 30 March 1990.

GEARY, WESLEY VAUGHAN. Fort Hood, Texas. Interviewed 21 February 1990.

GEIGER, LAWRENCE C. Tampa, Florida. Interview by Clark A. Foreid on 1 and 15 April 1994.

GRAY, RUDOLPH. Tampa, Florida. Interviewed 25 January 1990.

GREEN, HERBERT. Fifth Judicial Circuit, U.S. Army Trial Judiciary, APO, New York, NY. Letter and enclosures, 24 April 1990.

GROSSHEIM, PAUL. Department of Corrections, State of Iowa. Interviewed 2 February 1990.

GUIDERA, TOM. Satellite Beach, Florida. Interviewed 17 September 1998.

GUSTAFSON, KARL. Augusta, Georgia. Letter, 17 November 1990.

HART, WILLIAM. Commandant's Office, U.S. Army Disciplinary Barracks, Fort Leavenworth, Kansas. Interviewed 19 September 1990 and letter, 8 November 1990.

HATTON, JAMES. Veterans Administration Medical Center, St. Cloud, Minnesota. Interviewed 27 January 1990.

HUDAK, ANDREW. Yonkers, New York. Interviewed 13 October 1990 and letter, 8 January 1991.

JACKSON, NORWOOD. Office of Commissioner of Corrections for Westchester County, New York. Interviewed 30 March and 11 July 1990.

JACKSON, ROBERT. Texas State Prison, Huntsville, Texas. Letters, 28 February and 18 March 1990.

JAMES, JEREMIAH. West Jefferson Correctional Facility, Bessemer, Alabama. Interviewed 9 February 1990 and letter, 20 February 1990.

JONES, WILLY L. Washington, D.C. Interviewed 23 September 1990.

KEYES, WILLIAM. Jacksonville, Alabama. Interviewed 5 March 1990, 3 May 1990, 25 September 1990, 4 October 1998, 5 October 1998, and 5 December 1998.

KING, WAYNE. Fayetteville, Georgia. Interviewed 15 February 1990.

KRIES, CHARLES. Toledo, Ohio. Interviewed 19 January 1990.

LIBBY, BILLY. First United States Army Chaplain Office, Fort George G. Meade, Maryland. Interviewed 7 February 1990.

LUDWIG, RALPH E. Beaumont Army Medical Center, El Paso, Texas. Interviewed 21 February 1990.

MCCOTTER, O. LYNN. Office of the Director, New Mexico Department of Corrections. Interviewed 12 March 1990.

MCKEON, THOMAS. Indian Rocks Beach, Florida. Interviewed 23 September 1990.

MILDREN, FRANK T. Deputy Commanding General of USARV at the time of the riot. His remarks are taken from the Frank T. Mildren 1980 oral history report, U.S. Army Military History Institute, Carlisle Barracks, Carlisle, Pennsylvania.

MULLIN, SAM. Boston, Massachusetts. Interviewed 24 November 1998.

MURDOCK, EUGENE. Columbus, Georgia. Interviewed 2 April and 4 May 1990.

NELSON, IVAN. Palm Bay, Florida. Interviewed 2 April 1990.

NIX, CRISPUS. Warden's Office, Iowa State Penitentiary. Interviewed 7 March 1990.

PAYTON, GREGG. East Orange, New Jersey. Interviewed 7 April and 8 April 1990.

PEDERSON, JAMES. Waukesha, Wisconsin. Interviewed 22 September and 3 October 1990.

POWERS, MARION. North Little Rock, Arkansas. Interviewed 12 March 1990.

PRICE, WAYNE. Grant's Pass, Oregon. Interviewed 21 February 1990.

PROSSER, CLIFFORD. Birmingham, Alabama. Interviewed 25 February 1990.

SHIPPEE, VERNON. Savoy, Massachusetts. Interviewed 10 February 1990.

SMOOT, TERRY EDWARD. Oregon, Ohio. Interviewed 3 May 1990.

STAVEN, WAYNE R. Oak Creek, Wisconsin. Interviewed 15 May 1990.

STEEDLEY, KERRY. U.S. Army Aviation Center, Fort Rucker, Alabama. Interviewed 8 March 1990.

STEWART, RICHARD E. Atlanta, Georgia. Interviewed 26 February 1990.

STOVALL, GERALD. Nottoway Correctional Center, Burkeville, Virginia. Interviewed 29 April 1990.

SWIM, VERNON. Monument, Colorado. Interviewed 23 February 1990.

TROP, HERMAN. Jamestown, North Carolina. Interviewed 23 September 1990.

VAUGHAN, JAMES B. Dennison, Texas. Interviewed 16 February 1990.

WHITE, ALVIN, JR. Metro Correctional Institution, Atlanta, Georgia. Letters 27 January and 9 February 1990.

WOOTEN, FRANK. Leavenworth, Kansas. Interviewed 22 September 1990.

YUDESIS, BEN. Morrow, Georgia. Interviewed 29 March 1990.

# CONFINEMENT OFFICERS

This information has been pieced together entirely from the recollections of those interviewed. No official list of those who served as confinement officers at LBJ seems to exist, not at the Military Police Corps headquarters, nor with the MPC historian, nor at Department of Army level, nor in the Army's Military History archives. Thus this chart has time gaps. The names of some men who served in this position, particularly in the earliest years, were not discovered, and some of those who served as confinement officers, after a lapse of many years, could no longer remember the precise dates of their stay at LBJ. Memories grow vague with the passage of years, and therefore some dates derived from interviews are estimates only. An asterisk (*) marks the names of those interviewed for this study. Ranks are given as of the time they held the position of confinement officer.

| Name | Dates of Service |
|------|------------------|

**PERSHING FIELD**

| Name | Dates of Service |
|------|------------------|
| Capt. Walter Shumway | 1965 (?)–1966 (?) |
| Maj. Dale Groenenboom[1] | June 1966 (?)–January 1967 (?)[2] |

**USARVIS, LONG BINH**

| Name | Dates of Service |
|------|------------------|
| Maj. Dale Groenenboom | June 1966 (?)–January 1967 (?) |
| Lt. Col. Marvin D. Oberman | January 1967–July 1967 |
| *Lt. Col. George C. Deringer | 3 July 1967–4 July 1968 |
| *Maj. Norwood Jackson (Deringer's Deputy) | 4 July 1967–4 July 1968 |
| Lt. Col. Vernon D. Johnson | 5 July 1968–29 August 1968 |
| *Lt. Col. Eugene Murdock | 30 August 1968–mid-September 1968 |
| *Lt. Col. Herman Trop (Murdock's deputy) | A few days in September after the departure of Murdock |
| *Lt. Col. Ivan Nelson | 28 September 1968–November 1968 |
| *Lt. Col. William Keyes | November 1968–November 1969 |
| ———(Keyes's deputy) | November 1969–December 1969 |
| *Lt. Col. Willy Jones | January 1970 (?)–July 1970 (?) |
| *Lt. Col. Paul Grossheim | 14 July 1970–4 July 1971 |
| *Maj. James Pederson (Grossheim's deputy, served as a temporary confinement officer) | 5 July 1971–29 July 1971 |
| *Lt. Col. Eli Gardner | 30 July 1971–8 July 1972 |
| Maj. Doug Johnson | 9 July 1972–1 August 1972 (?) |

| Name | Dates of Service |
|---|---|
| Maj. Bruce Nagle | 2 August 1972 (?)–28 November 1972 (?) |
| *Capt. William Hart[3] | 29 November 1972–29 March 1973 |

### PERSHING FIELD

| | |
|---|---|
| *Capt. William Hart | 29 November 1972–29 March 1973 |

---

[1]Groenenboom's name and dates of service are entered twice because it was under his command that the stockade was moved from Pershing Field to Long Binh.

[2]Groenenboom fell ill with headaches. Army physicians determined he had a brain tumor, and in January 1967 he was evacuated to the continental United States for medical treatment.

[3]Hart's name and dates of service are entered twice because it was under his command that the stockade was closed down at Long Binh and returned to Pershing Field.

# BIBLIOGRAPHY

Transcripts of all interviews are located in the Long Binh Jail File, Cecil B. and Laura G. Currey Archive of Military History, Forsyth Library, Fort Hays State University, Hays, Kansas. Judy Salm, archivist. Lawrence Caylor, director.

Ackermann, Henry F. *The U.S. Army Chaplain Ministry in the Vietnam Conflict.* Washington, D.C.: U.S. Government Printing Office, 1989.

Berry, John Stevens. *Those Gallant Men: On Trial in Vietnam.* Novato, CA: Presidio Press, 1984.

*Bibliography List for Long Binh Jail.* U.S. Army Military History Institute, Carlisle Barracks, PA, 13 November 1989.

Congressional Black Caucus. *Racism in the Military: A New System for Rewards and Punishment.* Washington, D.C.: U.S. Government Printing Office, 1972.

Cortright, David. *Soldiers in Revolt.* New York: Doubleday Anchor, 1975.

Cortright, David. "Black GI Resistance During the Vietnam War," *Vietnam Generation* 2, no. 1 (1990): 51–64.

Department of Defense. *Report of the Task Force on the Administration of Military Justice.* 4 vols., Washington, D.C.: U.S. Government Printing Office, 1972.

Dunn, Carrol H. *Base Development in South Vietnam, 1965–1970*. Washington, D.C.: U.S. Department of the Army, 1972.

Long Binh Stockade. "Inspector General Investigation Concerning Alleged Brutality and Maltreatment at the US Army Vietnam Installation Stockade." 1969. Report of Investigation (Redacted), Stack 6, Vietnam Reference Files. Record Group 472. Records of the United States Army, Vietnam (USARV), National Archives, Washington, D.C.

Long Binh Stockade. Riot. 29–30 August 1968, Stack 6, Vietnam Reference Files. Record Group 472. CID Report of Investigations. Records of the United States Army, Vietnam (USARV). National Archives, Washington, D.C. These papers comprise the government's official investigation of the 1968 riot and are tagged with the code phrase "Blue Bell," indicating that they contained military information with sensitive political ramifications. Thus, they would circulate not only at the highest levels of the Pentagon, but copies would reach a few people at the White House and on Capitol Hill. Transcripts of testimonies were made by an investigative team from Detachment C, 8th MP Group (CID), Long Binh, Viet Nam. The team began its work immediately on 30 August, and the final report seems to have been forwarded to requisite authority on 23 January 1969. Testimonies of observers and participants, all taken at Long Binh, are transcribed on DA Forms 2823 and 2820. Some of these witness statements, fifty-six of them, were sent to me by Jack Crouchet and are complete in all respects. Others, sixty-four in number, came from the military and the names of most personnel had been removed from the documents. Comparing the reports sent by Crouchet with those received from the military revealed the names of most of those who gave testimony.

Mildren, General Frank T. Oral History Interview, U.S. Army Military History Institute, Carlisle Barracks, PA.

Rae, William R., Stephen B. Foreman, and Howard C. Olson. *Future Impact of Dissident Elements Within the Army on the Enforcement of Discipline, Law and Order*. Technical Paper #RAC-TP-441. McLean, VA: Research Analysis Corporation, 1972.

"Report of Investigation Concerning USARV Installation Stockade."
Sworn testimony taken from prisoners and facility personnel.
13 September 1968. Declassified 3 May 1990. Federal Records Center, National Archives, Washington, D.C.

Stein, Jeff. *A Murder in Wartime.* New York: St. Martin's Press, 1992.

"The Fall of a 'Lost Soldier.'" *Life,* 14 November 1969, 34–40.

Westmoreland, William C. *A Soldier Reports.* New York: Doubleday, 1976.

Williams, John W. "Race Riot at 'LBJ,'" and Crouchet, Jack. "Riot at the LBJ." *Vietnam Generation* 7, no. 1–2 (1995): 135–144.

# INDEX

120–21; cultural differences and, 61; guards and, 60–61; in Long Binh jail, 49–64; prisoners on, 86; and riot, 2–3, 24, 103, 110–12, 116–21, 125–26, 138, 157–58; sources of, 52–53
Recreational activities, 66, 83, 153, 167
Reese, prisoner, 117
Rehabilitation, Johnson on, 66
Religious services, 68–70, 161, 168
Rheault, Robert Bradley, xv, 148–51
Riot, 3–4, 100–101, 103–22; causes of, 110–11, 138; chaplains and, 161–62; Childress on, 1–3; cost of, 136, 138; course of, 126–28; of December 1966, 24–25; investigation of, 112, 137–38; of July 1971, 157–58, 164; plans for, 109, 111–12; resolution of, 123–39
Roberts, Ajary, 163
Rockholdt, guard, 118
Rodriques, prisoner, 107
Roll calls, black, 58–59
Ryan, Dennis, W., 119

Saigon, stockade at, 5
Schertzer, Mark P., 119
Search procedures, and riot, 111
Seliksky, Benson, 98
Shippee, Vernon, 9, 23–24
Shumway, Walter, 17, 180
Sick call, 76–77
Silver City, 27–29, 46, 142, 155
Skyhorse, Cy, 156–57
Smith, Billy, 63
Smith, Jody, 126
Smith, lieutenant colonel, 98
Smoot, Terry Edward, 41, 57, 63–64; on drug problem, 71; on riot, 157–58
Social workers, 34, 42; functions of, 66–67; as guards, 67–68; on racial tension, 56, 58
Sociopaths, management of, 61–63, 81
Soldiers, xii; characteristics of, 13, 17; treatment of, 109
Soloman, I., 107, 118
Son Tay raid, 43
Special courts, 12
Special Forces officers, xv, 148–51

Staff: on brutality, 92–94; fate of, ix–x; Johnson and, 84; number of, 50–51. See also Guards
Steedley, Kerry, 58, 67–69
Stovall, Gerald, 5, 31, 34; on brutality, 91–92; on causes of riot, 110; on escape plans, 105; on resolution of riot, 128, 132; on riot, 113, 116, 124–27
Strikes, 168
Suicide, 163; attempts at, 89
Sullivan, Dennis M., 119
Summary courts, 11–12
Swim, Vernon, 56, 68–69, 163; on brutality, 96; on drug problem, 70–71; on Gardner, 165; and Hensley, 164; on new Long Binh jail, 168–69

Tabler, Donald E., 117
Taft, Robert, 9
Talps, Ernest B., 123–25, 127
Terwilliger, private, 106–7
Tet Offensive, 54
Throckmorton, Paul F.. See Skyhorse, Cy
Thrumes, Leonard L., 119
Tilford, prisoner, 107
Tonkin Bay incident, 16
Trial procedures, 145–47
Trop, Herman, 84–85, 139, 180; and resolution of riot, 130–31, 133–34, 136
Troutman, Frank W., 112, 119, 125–26; trial of, 137
Trustees, 60; duties of, 33; pastimes of, 35

Uniform Code of Military Justice, 9–10; Article 13, 104; Article 32, 137–38
United States Army: discipline in, 9–10; investigation of brutality at Long Binh jail, 96–97, 100
United States Army Vietnam Installation (USARVIS), Long Binh, 173; bomb shelter, 21; chapel, 19, 23, 69, 168, 170; conditions in, 154–57, 160; construction of, 17–18, 20–23; daily routine, 24, 27–47; damages after riot, 138; defenses of, 19; at end of war, 170–72; exposé on, 163–64; food, 33, 35; hygiene, 35, 144;

# ABOUT THE AUTHOR

CECIL BARR CURREY is in phased retirement as a professor of military history at the University of South Florida in Tampa. In 1992 he retired with the rank of colonel from the U.S. Army Reserve in which he served as a chaplain. Author of numerous professional articles, encyclopedia and dictionary entries, and book chapters, he has also written twelve books. Those that deal with Viet Nam include *Self-Destruction: The Disintegration and Decay of the United States Army During the Viet Nam Era* (1981) and *Edward Lansdale: The Unquiet American* (1988). His last book, *Victory at Any Cost: The Genius of Viet Nam's General Vo Nguyen Giap* (1997), received the 1997 President's Book Prize of the Association of Third World Studies.